Religions
of the World

Christianity

William W. Lace

LUCENT BOOKS
An imprint of Thomson Gale, a part of The Thomson Corporation

THOMSON
———— * ————™
GALE

Detroit • New York • San Francisco • San Diego • New Haven, Conn. • Waterville, Maine • London • Munich

THOMSON
━━━━★━━━━ ™
GALE

© 2005 Thomson Gale, a part ot The Thomson Corporation.

Thomson and Star Logo are trademarks and Gale and Lucent Books are registered trademarks used herein under license.

For more information, contact
Lucent Books
27500 Drake Rd.
Farmington Hills, MI 48331-3535
Or you can visit our Internet site at http://www.gale.com

LIBRARY OF CONGRESS CATALOGING-IN-PUBLICATION DATA

Lace, William W.
    Christianity / by William W. Lace.
      p. cm. — (Religions of the world)
    Includes bibliographical references and index.
    Contents: Jesus of Nazareth—Paul, the master builder—Persecution to prominence—Heresy and schism—Reformation and counter-reformation—Expansion and enlightenment—Beliefs and worship—Christianity in the new millennium.
    ISBN 1-59018-141-7 (hardcover: alk. paper)
    1. Christianity. I. Title II. Series: Religions of the world (San Diego, Calif.)
  BR121.3.L33 2004
  230—dc22

                                              2004010844

Printed in the United States of America

Contents

Foreword   4

Introduction   He Who Will Come   6

Chapter 1   Jesus of Nazareth   10

Chapter 2   Paul, the Master Builder   22

Chapter 3   Persecution to Prominence   31

Chapter 4   Heresy and Schism   44

Chapter 5   Power and Perversion   56

Chapter 6   Reformation and
               Counter-Reformation   68

Chapter 7   Expansion and Enlightenment   80

Chapter 8   Beliefs and Worship   93

Chapter 9   Christianity in the New
               Millennium   104

Notes   117

For Further Reading   120

Works Consulted   121

Index   124

Picture Credits   128

About the Author   128

Foreword

Religion has always been a central component of human culture, though its form and practice have changed through time. Ancient people lived in a world they could not explain or comprehend. Their world consisted of an environment controlled by vague and mysterious powers attributed to a wide array of gods. Artifacts dating to a time before recorded history suggest that the religion of the distant past reflected this world, consisting mainly of rituals devised to influence events under the control of these gods.

The steady advancement of human societies brought about changes in religion as in all other things. Through time, religion came to be seen as a system of beliefs and practices that gave meaning to—or allowed acceptance of—anything that transcended the natural or the known. And, the belief in many gods ultimately was replaced in many cultures by the belief in a Supreme Being.

As in the distant past, however, religion still provides answers to timeless questions: How, why, and by whom was the universe created? What is the ultimate meaning of human life? Why is life inevitably followed by death? Does the human soul continue to exist after death, and if so, in what form? Why is there pain and suffering in the world, and why is there evil?

In addition, all the major world religions provide their followers with a concrete and clearly stated ethical code. They offer a set of moral instructions, defining virtue and evil and what is required to achieve goodness. One of these universal moral codes is compassion toward others above all else. Thus, Judaism, Christianity, Islam, Hinduism, Buddhism, Confucianism, and Taoism each teach a version of the so-called golden rule, or in the words of Jesus Christ, "As ye would that men should do to you, do ye also to them likewise" (Luke 6:31). For example, Confucius instructed his disciples to "never impose on others what you would not choose for yourself" (*Analects:* 12:2). The Hindu epic poem, Mahabharata,

4

identifies the core of all Hindu teaching as not doing unto others what you do not wish done to yourself. Similarly Muhammad declared that no Muslim could be a true believer unless he desires for his brother no less than that which he desires for himself.

It is ironic, then, that although compassionate concern for others forms the heart of all the major religions' moral teachings, religion has also been at the root of countless conflicts throughout history. It has been suggested that much of the appeal that religions hold for humankind lies in their unswerving faith in the truth of their particular vision. Throughout history, most religions have shared a profound confidence that their interpretation of life, God, and the universe is the right one, thus giving their followers a sense of certainty in an uncertain and often fragile existence. Given the assurance displayed by most religions regarding the fundamental correctness of their teachings and practices, it is perhaps not surprising that religious intolerance has fueled disputes and even full-scale wars between peoples and nations time and time again, from the Crusades of medieval times to the current bloodshed in Northern Ireland and the Middle East.

Today, as violent religious conflicts trouble many parts of our world, it has become more important than ever to learn about the similarities as well as the differences between faiths. One of the most effective ways to accomplish this is by examining the beliefs, customs, and values of various religions. In the Religions of the World series, students will find a clear description of the core creeds, rituals, ethical teachings, and sacred texts of the world's major religions. In-depth explorations of how these faiths changed over time, how they have influenced the social customs, laws, and education of the countries in which they are practiced, and the particular challenges each one faces in coming years are also featured.

Extensive quotations from primary source materials, especially the core scriptures of each faith, and a generous number of secondary source quotations from the works of respected modern scholars are included in each volume in the series. It is hoped that by gaining insight into the faiths of other peoples and nations, students will not only gain a deeper appreciation and respect for different religious beliefs and practices, but will also gain new perspectives on and understanding of their own religious traditions.

He Who Will Come

Christianity, the faith that today takes in one of every three people on earth, is based on a message of love and peace preached by a man who, tradition holds, was a humble carpenter, born in a stable in a remote backwater of the Roman Empire. Christianity's origins, however, extend further—to a captive people who longed not for a man of peace but for a mighty conqueror to lead them to freedom.

About two thousand years before the birth of Jesus of Nazareth, the patriarch Abraham, according to the book of Genesis in the Bible, led his tribe from an area just north of the Persian Gulf to the land of Canaan on the eastern coast of the Mediterranean Sea. These people, known as the Hebrews, brought with them the belief, unique for that time and place, that there is only one God.

The Bible tells how Abraham's grandson, Jacob, wrestled throughout the night with an angel and was renamed Israel, meaning "God has striven." Jacob had twelve sons, who became the founders of the twelve tribes of the people who called themselves the Children of Israel, or Israelites.

Generations later, the Israelites achieved their greatest extent of power under King David and his son, Solomon. After Solomon's death in 922 B.C., however, internal dissention divided the kingdom. The ten northern tribes became the Kingdom of Israel; the two southern tribes, the Kingdom of Judah, from which come the terms *Judaism* and *Jew*, although both the Israelites and Jews shared the same religion.

The two kingdoms, caught between the major powers of Assyria to the north and Egypt to the south, would not endure. In about 735 B.C. the Assyrians invaded Israel and carried off most of the people. Israel, as a nation, would cease to exist until modern times. More than a century later, Babylon, successor to Assyria, invaded Judah, destroyed

Jacob wrestles with an angel in this painting by Rembrandt. The angel gave Jacob the name of Israel, and his descendants, the Jews, became known as the Children of Israel.

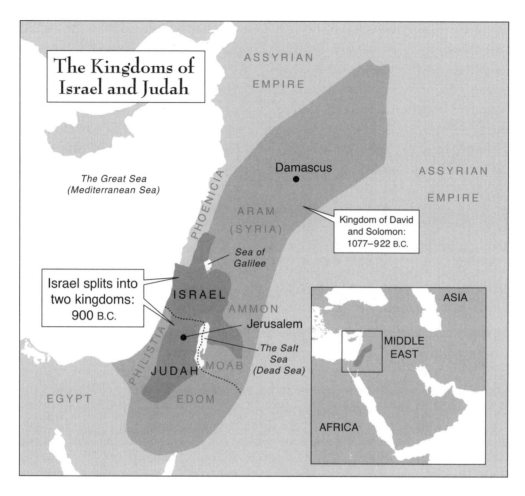

The Kingdoms of Israel and Judah

ASSYRIAN EMPIRE

The Great Sea (Mediterranean Sea)

PHOENICIA

Damascus

ASSYRIAN EMPIRE

ARAM (SYRIA)

Kingdom of David and Solomon: 1077–922 B.C.

Sea of Galilee

Israel splits into two kingdoms: 900 B.C.

ISRAEL

AMMON

Jerusalem

PHILISTIA

The Salt Sea (Dead Sea)

JUDAH

MOAB

EGYPT

EDOM

ASIA

MIDDLE EAST

AFRICA

the great temple of Solomon, and marched most of this remaining population of Jews into captivity.

The so-called Babylonian Captivity lasted only about fifty years, but it had enormous consequences. First, to maintain their religion despite the destruction of their center of worship, the Jews developed a practice of strict observance of the laws supposedly handed down by God. Second, they formed a belief in a deliverer, a savior who would free them from their bondage. They called this longed-for savior the messiah, or "anointed one."

The Prophets

This longing was put into words by a series of prophets. Of these, it was Isaiah who most clearly forecast what was to become the basis of Christianity, writing (7:14), "Therefore the Lord himself shall give you a sign; Behold, a virgin shall conceive, and bear a Son, and shall call his name Immanuel [meaning 'God with us']." This child, furthermore, would be destined for greatness. As Isaiah wrote (9:6), "For unto us a child is born, unto us a son is given: and the government shall be upon his shoulders: and his name shall be called wonderful, counselor, the mighty God, the everlasting father, the Prince of Peace."

Isaiah even forecast that this messiah would suffer at the hands of enemies and that through his suffering humanity might benefit. He wrote (53:5), "But he was wounded for our transgressions, he was bruised for our iniquities: the chastisement of our peace was upon him; and with his stripes [from being whipped] we are healed."

The Jews were restored to their kingdom, renamed Judea, in 539 B.C. but the golden age of David and Solomon was never regained. After a time of prosperity, Judea fell under the domination of others. Alexander the Great of Macedonia conquered much of the eastern Mediterranean region, including Judea, in 332 B.C. Then, after the empire founded by Alexander broke apart, a new conqueror appeared—Rome.

The legions of the Roman general Pompey conquered Judea and the other parts of the region known as Palestine in 63 B.C. and installed puppet kings. Once again, as they had five hundred years before in Babylon, the Jews prayed for the messiah to deliver them. It was into this world and time that Jesus of Nazareth was born. He would change the world, but not in the manner some might have expected or hoped.

chapter one

Jesus of Nazareth

Little is known or documented about the life of Jesus of Nazareth, on whose teachings Christianity is based. No one knows for certain exactly when he was born, when he died, or how long his ministry lasted. The few accounts of his life were written decades after his death, and layers of legend may have obscured the facts.

Jesus's identity and purpose in life were unclear even to those closest to him. He was hailed as the promised messiah but never claimed to be such. He never explicitly said he was the son of God. He never announced an intention to start a new religion, although he encouraged people to follow him.

Most of what is known—or what Christians believe—about Jesus's life comes from the four New Testament books known as Gospels. These narratives are attributed to Matthew and John—two of Jesus's twelve original disciples —and to first-century Christians Mark and Luke, although the authorship of all four is by no means certain.

Matthew and Luke, the only Gospels to recount Jesus's birth, disagree on the date. Matthew puts it sometime before the death of King Herod in 4 B.C., but Luke ties it to a Roman census that took place in A.D. 6.

Christian tradition states that Jesus's mother, Mary, was a virgin who was made pregnant by the Holy Spirit—the

The Virgin Birth

One of the most controversial aspects of Christianity—taken on faith by believers, doubted by skeptics—is the account of the birth of Jesus to Mary, a virgin. The earliest Christian writings do not mention it, and it does not appear until Luke's Gospel, thought to have been written about A.D. 80.

Some scholars think Luke, and the author of Matthew's gospel afterward, inserted the story in order to make it seem like Jesus had fulfilled the prophecy of Isaiah (7:14) that "a virgin shall conceive and bear a son." They point out that the Hebrew word Isaiah used, *almah*, can mean "young woman" and question why, if the prophet really meant virgin, he did not use the specific Hebrew word *betulah*. Defenders of the story counter that *almah*, when used in other places in the Old Testament, clearly means a virgin.

Many people say it is possible to doubt the story of the virgin birth and still remain a faithful Christian. A survey in 2002 of Church of England clergy showed that 27 percent privately doubt the story. One priest, who did not want his name used because of possible objections from church leaders, told the *Sydney (Australia) Morning Herald*, "There was nothing special about his birth or childhood—it was his adult life that was extraordinary."

This fifteenth-century Italian fresco shows Mary holding the baby Jesus. The Bible claims Mary was a virgin at the time of Jesus's birth, a tradition some Christians question.

power of God. Some scholars claim the story of the virgin birth arose long after Jesus's time so as to fulfill Isaiah's prophecy. Christians, however, consider the virgin birth as one of the foundations of the religion, since it gives Jesus both a human and divine nature. As historian Roland Herbert Bainton writes:

> Whether fact, legend, or myth, the birth stories enshrine two themes, celebration in heaven and rejection on earth. The angels sang, but because "there was no room for them in the inn," [Luke 2:7] the Savior had to be born in a stable. . . . To be sure, according to the Scripture, wise men came from the East to do homage to the new-born King of the Jews, but . . . of his own people only shepherds gathered about the crib. . . . The birth presaged [foretold] the Passion [Jesus's death].[1]

The Baptism

The Gospels say almost nothing about Jesus's childhood and youth but go into much more detail beginning with his baptism by his cousin, John, in the Jordan River. John preached that the kingdom of God, foretold by the ancient prophets, was at hand. Many he baptized thought John was the promised messiah, but he denied it, saying (Matthew 3:11), "I baptize you with water for repentance, but he who is coming after me is mightier than I, whose sandals I am not worthy to carry; he will baptize you with the Holy Spirit and with fire." To Christians, John was saying that Jesus was the fulfillment of the Old Testament prophecies.

Luke states that Jesus was about thirty years old when he began his ministry. The gospels give no hint as to what led him to take up the life of a wandering preacher. He presumably had some knowledge, perhaps from what he interpreted as messages from God, that he had somehow been chosen as God's instrument.

As had John, Jesus took his message directly to the people—the ordinary farmers and villagers of Galilee, far away from the center of power to the south in Jerusalem. In so doing, writes theology professor Gerald Hall, he was making a point:

> He departs from accepted practice by choosing his own disciples and enjoying table-fellowship with tax-collectors, prostitutes and sinners. The ease of his relationship with women also raised eyebrows. Above all, the

This painting by Leonardo da Vinci shows Jesus being baptized by his cousin John the Baptist. Soon afterward, Jesus began his ministry.

historical Jesus emerges as one who speaks and acts with great personal authority by ministering to social outcasts, claiming to forgive sins and speaking of his own relationship with God in the most intimate terms.[2]

The Kingdom of God

Jesus's theme was also similar to that of John—the kingdom of God was near and people should repent their sins and resolve to lead more godly lives. But what was this kingdom of God? The concept sounded threatening to Roman and Jewish officials and was puzzling even to Jesus's disciples.

The preaching of Jesus called for reform, but he said from the very first that his purpose was not to overthrow the established order, as

13

The Historical Jesus

Historians have long searched for hard evidence supporting the Gospel accounts of Jesus's life. Theologian Paul Tillich, in "The Search for the Historical Jesus" (found in The Church Theology Reader, *edited by Alister McGrath), says it makes no difference:*

"Faith cannot rest on such unsure ground. . . . There is another possible answer, which, though not false, is misleading. This is to say that the historical foundation of Christianity is an essential element of the Christian faith itself and that this faith, through its own power, can overrule skeptical possibilities within historical criticism. It can, it is maintained, guarantee the existence of Jesus of Nazareth and at least the essentials in the biblical picture. But we must analyze the answer carefully, for it is ambiguous. The problem is: Exactly what can faith guarantee? And the inevitable answer is that faith can guarantee only its own foundation, namely, the appearance of that reality which has created the faith. This reality is the New Being, who conquers existential estrangement and thereby makes faith possible. This alone faith is able to guarantee—and that because its own existence is identical with the presence of the New Being. . . . It guarantees a personal life in which the New Being has conquered the old being. But it does not guarantee his name to be Jesus of Nazareth. Historical doubt concerning the existence and life of someone with this name cannot be overruled. He might have had another name. . . . Whatever his name, the new Being was and is actual in this man."

represented by the laws of Judaism. Rather, he said (Matthew 5:17), "Think not that I have come to abolish the law and the prophets; I have come not to abolish them but to fulfill them." Nevertheless, writes theologian John Crosson, "the phrase 'kingdom of God' could easily have been understood in an apocalyptic [prophesying destruction] sense at the time of Jesus. . . . The specific content could be quite open or even vague, for example, with or without an armed revolt, with or without a messiah, with our without a cosmic destruction."[3]

That law had become an exceedingly complex set of regulations and its adherents increasingly rigid in its observance. By Jesus's time, the law had become all important. The leaders of Judaism believed that strict obedience to the law in all its many forms was all that was necessary to find favor in God's sight. Religion for many had become more a matter of how people behaved outwardly rather than what they felt inwardly.

While he did not reject the law, Jesus taught that there was a higher power—love of God and love for one another. "On these two commandments," he said (Matthew 22:40), "hang all the law and the prophets." He drew a distinction between the laws of God and the layers of rules that had been piled upon them. Keeping the commandments, he said, was not enough. Rather, he said, people should love and forgive their enemies just as God loves and forgives them.

God's Love

The core of Jesus's message was that God has an infinite capacity for love and forgiveness and that all people, in their daily lives, should reflect this love. He rejected the legalistic aspects of Jewish law as embodied in the "eye for eye, tooth for tooth" prescriptions of the Old Testament (Exodus 21:24). Rather, he said,

A Byzantine mosaic shows Jesus conferring a blessing with one hand while holding a sacred text with the other.

people should love and forgive their enemies and (Luke 6:29) "bless those who curse you, pray for those who abuse you." Just as God loves you, he preached, you should love others and let this love be reflected in your actions.

This message was simple and direct, and it had great appeal for Jesus's listeners, who came to hear him in increasing numbers. He did not employ intricate theological arguments supported by scripture but instead often employed parables, or stories, using examples from people's everyday lives to illustrate his themes. These parables would have been more understandable to Jesus's listeners, but they may have had another purpose. Gerald Hall writes:

> Without rejecting the value of moral and allegorical interpretations, modern scholarship . . . has focused attention on the organic unity and underlying structure of parables. It also asks how parables function in relation to the central message of the reign of God in Jesus' teaching and ministry. . . . Jesus challenges his hearers to a new mode of being in the world. He does not simply talk about the reign of God but seeks to give the listener an anticipatory experience

of what the reign of God is like in the here and now. Parables play on the relationship between the familiar and the strange; they reverse our ordinary way of experiencing the world and shock us into a type of reversed consciousness. Parables induce us to look at our lives and make decisions about our futures.[4]

The Disciples

As his following grew, Jesus found it necessary to enlist helpers. He did not seek out people of influence or wealth or those trained in law or theology. Rather, he chose ordinary men much like himself and those to whom he had been preaching. The disciples, however, were much more than mere assistants. Jesus explicitly gave them the authority to preach and to act in his name. Even so, none of his instructions to them indicated a wish or intention to begin a new religion outside of Judaism.

Jesus went out of his way to preach that the virtues most prized by God were not those most highly valued by Jewish leaders of the time: knowledge of the law, authority, outward piety, and affluence. The meek and merciful, he said, are truly righteous —not the religious elite. Furthermore, he told the people (Matthew

Fates of the Apostles

The men Jesus of Nazareth chose to help in his ministry were truly a varied lot. They included fishermen, a tax collector, and a lawyer. Nothing is known about some of them except their names.

The original twelve disciples were Peter, Andrew, James the Greater, James the Lesser, John, Thomas, Jude, Philip, Bartholomew, Matthew, Simon, and Judas Iscariot. Many were to die violent deaths, the first of whom was Judas, who tradition says hanged himself after betraying Jesus to the Jewish authorities.

More is known about the subsequent career of Peter than about any of the other disciples. He traveled to Rome and was executed there in A.D. 64 as part of Nero's persecution. Tradition says he was crucified upside down at his own wish, since he felt unworthy to die in exactly the same manner as Jesus.

Matthew and Simon likewise were crucified, and John is said to have been killed in a pot of boiling oil. James the Greater was executed in Judea after returning from preaching in Spain, where he is honored as that country's patron saint.

Thomas is supposed to have gone as far as India, founding a church there that was still active when Portuguese missionaries arrived there in the 1500s.

5:20), "Unless your righteousness exceeds that of the scribes and Pharisees, you will never enter the kingdom of heaven."

Such statements made the scribes and Pharisees, two of the major powers in Judaism, very unhappy. The third Judaic force were the Sadducees, priests who served in the temple in Jerusalem and who made up the ultimate religious authority, the Sanhedrin.

As Jesus's fame spread, these powerful groups became increasingly wary of him. By preaching that love of God and neighbor was higher than the law, he undercut their authority. Moreover, by encouraging people to share their wealth directly with the poor, he threatened their income from gifts to the temple.

Jesus also did not directly challenge the secular authorities. He acknowledged the legitimacy of earthly governments. He did not preach revolution. The kingdom of God, he said, was not an earthly kingdom in which the Roman government would be overthrown. Instead, it was a kingdom, reigned over by God, that existed in heaven and in the hearts of people who were in peace and harmony with God and neighbor. He did not say that wealth was inherently evil, but that seeking wealth diverted people from seeking God.

Healing

Jesus's preaching was enough to get him in trouble with the Jewish au-thorities, and even more so when he demonstrated his power by healing the sick. Such displays left him open to charges of witchcraft. As theo-logian Bruce Shelly writes, Jesus realized this but thought such demonstrations were necessary: "Jesus hinted that the rule of God was already present in his own per-son. And he offered proof to the

Jesus raises Lazarus from the dead in this painting by Peter Paul Rubens. Jewish authorities saw Jesus's miraculous powers as a threat to their own supremacy.

point. His miracles of healing were apparently not just marvels, they were signs, the powers of the age to come already manifest in the present age."[5]

So it was that when, as related in John's gospel, Jesus raised his friend Lazarus from the dead, his enemies, led by the high priest Caiaphas, determined to get rid of him. The Pharisees said (John 11:48), "If we let him go on thus, every one will believe in him, and the Romans will come and destroy both our holy place and our nation."

According to the Gospels, Jesus knew what was in store for him. As they prepared to go to Jerusalem for the Jewish feast of Passover, commemorating the Hebrews' deliverance from slavery in Egypt, he told his disciples (Mark 10:33), "Behold, we are going up to Jerusalem; and the Son of man will be delivered to the chief priests and the scribes, and they will condemn him to death, and deliver him to the Gentiles [non-Jews, in this case the Romans]."

Jesus's Sacrifice

The Gospels make it clear that Jesus not only knew his destiny but welcomed it. Much as the Jews sacrificed animals in the temple in order to please God and atone for their sins, Jesus offered himself for a sacrifice, Christians believe, taking on the sins of all humankind. His death, therefore, would wipe humanity's slate clean and open the way for God's kingdom on earth. As explained by theology professor Alan Scholes:

> God the Father reached back in time and took the spiritual death [human sins] that had been generated by Adam [in the Garden of Eden] and those who came after him and placed it on Jesus Christ. Then ... God looked forward in time and took all the spiritual death generated by you and me and all the other men and women who will be born until the end of time and put that death on Jesus, too.[6]

Jesus underscored the theme of sacrifice on the night before he was arrested. During the traditional Jewish ceremonial Passover supper, he asked the disciples to take bread and wine, telling them (Matthew 26:28) that it was his body and blood, "poured out for many for the forgiveness of sins." This part of what came to be known as the Last Supper would later be incorporated into Christian worship.

Later that night, when Jesus was in a garden with his disciples, a

The Last Supper is shown in a fifteenth-century Italian fresco. This final meal with his disciples is commemorated in the Christian ceremony known as the Eucharist.

crowd sent by the high priest came to arrest him. It was led by one of the disciples, Judas Iscariot. Judas may have been part of yet another segment of Judaism known as the Zealots, revolutionaries who believed that the Jews should rebel against Rome and set up a government based entirely on Jewish law. If this is true, Judas might have believed that Jesus was destined to lead this rebellion and betrayed him in order to bring about a crisis that would set it off.

After his arrest, Jesus was taken before the high priest and asked if he was the messiah, the son of God. Jesus did not answer directly, but said (Mark 15:2), "You have said so," but then added that his accusers should someday see him at the right hand of God. That was enough for the Sanhedrin, which convicted him of blasphemy and condemned him to death.

Pontius Pilate

Only the Romans, however, could carry out a death sentence. Jesus was taken to the Roman governor, Pontius Pilate, who did not understand what the uproar was about. He considered it an internal Jewish matter. Probably eager to avoid a riot, Pilate finally gave in to the Sanhedrin and ordered Jesus to be executed by crucifixion, a degrading punishment the Romans usually reserved for slaves, rebels, and common criminals.

Jesus was first whipped by Roman soldiers, thus fulfilling Isaiah's prophecy about stripes. The soldiers pressed a crown made of thorns on his head and mocked him as "King of the Jews." They then led him out of Jerusalem to a nearby hill called Golgotha, nailed his hands and feet to a wooden cross, and set the cross upright between those of two robbers. After Jesus died, his body was wrapped in a white shroud and placed in a cavelike tomb that had been carved out of rock. Since the Jewish authorities feared his disciples would try to steal the body, they had the Romans post a guard.

Two days later, on Sunday, some women followers of Jesus came to anoint the body in accordance with Jewish custom. They found the Roman guards asleep and the stone sealing the tomb rolled back. According to scripture, when they entered the tomb, the women saw an angel who said to them (Mark 16:6), "Do not be amazed; you seek Jesus of Nazareth, who was crucified. He has risen, he is not here; see the place where they laid him."

Jesus's resurrection from the dead, one of the core beliefs of Christianity, had been foretold in the Old Testament. Isaiah had written (53:10), "When he makes himself an offering for sin, he shall see his offspring, he shall prolong his days." Jesus had also forecast the event, saying he would destroy the temple and rebuild it in three days. Although his enemies interpreted this statement as rebellious, Christians believe Jesus meant that he would die and in three days live again, thus bringing about a new era for humanity and a new hope for salvation.

For Jesus's disciples, however, his death was scarcely the start of anything magnificent, but a catastrophe. This small, huddled band of frightened men feared that they might well suffer a fate similar to that of their leader. No one, least of all they, could have predicted that what they thought was the end was only the beginning.

chapter | two

Paul, the Master Builder

When Jesus of Nazareth died on the cross, the Jewish and Roman officials doubtless thought they had heard the last of him. It was due chiefly to the faith and determination of his followers, particularly Paul of Tarsus, that the message of Jesus would be carried throughout much of the known world and what was still a splinter group would be shaped into a religion.

Jesus's execution must have seemed to his disciples to be the destruction of everything they had hoped for. Even though Jesus had said they were to carry out his work, they were at a loss as to how to proceed. In the days following the crucifixion, they were confused, leaderless, and fearful of their own deaths.

The book of Mark tells how, even after one of the women at the tomb, Mary Magdalene, told the disciples she had seen the risen Jesus, they would not believe her. Later, he appeared to two unnamed disciples, but still the rest would not believe. It was only when Jesus appeared to all eleven remaining disciples that they took hope.

According to the book of the Acts of the Apostles, Jesus lived among his disciples for forty days after the crucifixion, after which he was lifted to heaven. The author, thought to have been Luke, makes it clear that Jesus was not a spirit or ghost. He had the disciples touch him to demonstrate that he was real. He ate and drank with them.

He preached to the disciples about God's kingdom. He also, in what some take as the beginnings of the Christian church, told them that it was now their duty to carry on his work. He charged them (Mark 16:15–16), "Go into all the world and preach the gospel to the whole creation. He who believes and is baptized will be saved; but he who does not believe will be condemned."

Time of Confusion

Jesus's departure left his disciples with no clear understanding of what they were supposed to do or how they were to accomplish it. The kingdom of God was coming, they had been told, but when? Who would the kingdom include? What had Jesus meant by "all the world"? They stayed out of sight, meeting secretly to decide how to proceed, and it was at one of these meetings, some scholars contend, that Christianity was born.

The occasion was the holy day of Pentecost, fifty days after the Jewish Passover. The disciples were gathered in a room when, according to Acts (2:2), "a sound came from heaven like the rush of a mighty wind, and it filled all the house where they were

A seventeenth-century French painting shows tongues of fire descending on Jesus's disciples. The event is considered to be the beginning of Christianity.

sitting." Tongues of fire descended and rested on the head of each man, whereupon they began speaking in languages hitherto unknown to them. The disciples took this as a sign from God that they were, indeed, to emerge from the shadows and publicly proclaim Jesus's message.

From this time on their role became less that of disciples, or followers, than of apostles, or messengers. The first to preach was Simon, whom Jesus had renamed Peter, from the Greek word for "rock," and upon whom he said his kingdom would be built. He told the people of Jerusalem that Jesus had been raised from the dead by God, and that if they repented and were baptized in Jesus's name, they, too, would have everlasting life. About three thousand people were baptized in a single day, according to the book of Acts.

The Jewish Question

As the infant church grew, conflict arose. The earliest Christians still considered themselves Jews, and the Jewish establishment also considered the movement a sect of Judaism, not a separate religion. Thus the first problem confronting Christianity was whether or not Gentiles, or non-Jews, could join and, if so, whether they first had to become Jews.

According to Acts, Peter had a vision in which, after he protested that he had never eaten anything considered unclean by Jewish law, a voice said (Acts 10:15), "What God has cleansed, you must not call common." Peter took the vision to mean that baptism was open to all believers and that people did not have to be or become Jews to be baptized. His decision, which the other apostles accepted somewhat reluctantly, was crucial for the growth of Christianity.

As the movement grew, some sort of organization became necessary. These early Christians believed that Jesus would return soon, perhaps in only weeks, to establish his kingdom. In the meantime, they gave up all they owned and lived in a communal setting. To help govern and distribute goods, seven men were elected to assist the apostles, thus becoming the first deacons.

One of the deacons, Stephen, began to preach as ably and eloquently as any of the apostles. So forceful was he that he quickly drew the attention and then the wrath of Jewish authorities. Brought before the Sanhedrin, Stephen lashed out, saying (Acts 7:52–53), "Which of the prophets did not your fathers persecute? And they killed those who announced beforehand the

Death in the Arena

Christianity came to the attention of most Romans when, in A.D. 64, Emperor Nero accused members of the new religion of starting a fire that destroyed about one-third of the city. To punish the Christians—and to help take the Romans' minds off the fire's destruction—Nero had them tortured and killed before crowds in an arena. The Roman historian Tacitus, writing a few years afterward, gave this description, found at www.wsu.edu:

"Therefore, in order to abolish that rumor, Nero falsely accused and executed with the most exquisite punishments those people called Christians, who were infamous for their abominations. . . . And perishing they were additionally made

into sport: they were killed by dogs by having the hides of beasts attached to them, or they were nailed to crosses or set aflame, and, when the daylight passed away, they were used as nighttime lamps. . . . Even though they were clearly guilty and merited being made the most recent example of the consequences of crime, people began to pity these sufferers, because they were consumed not for the public good but on account of the fierceness of one man."

A marble bust of Nero, who had Christians publicly tortured and executed.

coming of the Righteous One, whom you have now betrayed and murdered, you who received the law as delivered by angels and did not keep it." When he said he saw a vision of

Jesus standing at the right hand of God, he was found guilty of blasphemy, hauled outside the city walls, and stoned to death, the first of many thousands of Christians who would die for their faith in centuries to come.

Saul of Tarsus

Before they killed Stephen, his executioners laid their robes at the feet of a young colleague for safekeeping. His name was Saul, and he was destined to be perhaps the most important figure in the history of Christianity other than Jesus. Without him, the Christian church would not exist in its present form and, indeed, might not exist at all.

A native of Tarsus in modern-day Turkey, Saul had inherited Roman citizenship from his father, a well-to-do tent maker who, though not a Roman, may have been granted citizenship for some act of service to the government. Although a devout Jew, Saul had been influenced by Hellenistic, or Greek, culture and used a Greek name, Paul, when in the company of non-Jews.

Paul was passionate in whatever he did, and at the time of Stephen's death his great passion was the per-

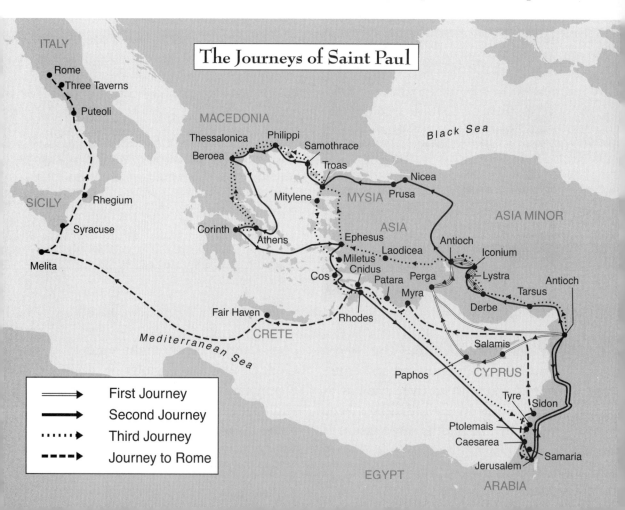

The Journeys of Saint Paul

ITALY
Rome
Three Taverns
Puteoli
MACEDONIA
Thessalonica   Philippi
Beroea   Samothrace
                        Troas
                                    Nicea
SICILY   Rhegium   Mitylene   MYSIA   Prusa
                                ASIA
Syracuse   Corinth   Ephesus   Antioch
                        Athens   Laodicea   Iconium
Melita   Miletus
                        Cos   Cnidus   Patara   Perga   Lystra
                                            Myra   Tarsus   Antioch
                        Fair Haven   Derbe
Mediterranean Sea   CRETE   Rhodes
                                            Salamis
                        Paphos   CYPRUS
                                    Tyre   Sidon
                        Ptolemais
                        Caesarea   Samaria
                        Jerusalem
EGYPT
                        ARABIA

Black Sea
ASIA MINOR

→ First Journey
→ Second Journey
·····▶ Third Journey
---▶ Journey to Rome

secution of Jesus's followers. After the stoning of Stephen, Paul eagerly volunteered to go to the city of Damascus to search out Christians there. On the way, however, according to chapter 9 of Acts, a bright light flashed around him, rendering him blind. As he fell to the ground he heard a voice saying, "Saul, Saul, why do you persecute me?" When Paul asked who called him, the voice answered, "I am Jesus, whom you are persecuting; but rise and enter the city, and you will be told what you are to do."

The author of Acts goes on to tell how Paul was led into Damascus. There a Christian named Ananias was instructed by the voice of Jesus to place his hands on Paul in the name of the Holy Spirit, "for he is a chosen instrument of mine to carry my name before the Gentiles and kings and the sons of Israel." Paul's sight was restored and he was baptized in Jesus's name.

Paul's Zeal

Jesus could have found no better messenger. Paul now showed the same zeal spreading Christianity as he had persecuting those who followed it. He was utterly fearless, facing angry mobs and hostile officials with absolute certainty as to the truth of what he preached. He was tireless, traveling about eight thousand miles on land and sea in three missionary journeys over a twelve-year span.

More important than his courage or stamina, however, was Paul's intellect. His solid grounding in both the Jewish law and classical Greek philosophy enabled him to more than hold his own in debates with adversaries within and outside of the church. He was able to argue with the Pharisees from the standpoint of a Jew and to reason with adherents of various Greek philosophies in such a way as to make Christianity a logical extension of their own beliefs. Such was his breadth of knowledge that he acknowledged his ability (1 Corinthians 9:22) to be "all things to all men, that I might by all means save some."

Every city Paul visited had a Jewish synagogue, and it was there that he would begin his work. His listeners varied in their reactions. Some were outraged, as in Iconium, from which he and his companion Barnabus had to flee for their lives. Others, such as the congregation in Antioch, "spoke to them [Paul and Barnabas] and urged them to continue in the grace of God" (Acts 13:14).

Paul was able to convert large numbers of people—some Jews, but most Gentiles—and leave behind him not a scattering of believers, but established churches. Among others, Paul founded congregations in Corinth, Philippi, and throughout the region of Galatia.

Paul's Epistles

These churches, once Paul had departed them, were constantly in his thoughts. He fretted over them like a parent over children, sending letters to the congregations in which he variously encouraged, scolded, warned, challenged, or praised them as he felt the occasion warranted. These letters, or epistles, attributed to Paul and sent to his churches as well as to his colleagues Timothy, Titus, and Philemon constitute the bulk of the New Testament and laid the foundations for Christianity as an organized faith.

While Paul's epistles dealt in part with mundane matters—settling arguments, laying down qualifications for bishops—they also presented his views of who and what Jesus was and what his life, death, and resurrection meant to humanity. Written earlier than any of the gospels, they were widely circulated and became the standard reference for those who came after Paul.

Paul's fundamental view was that Jesus was neither wholly human nor wholly divine, but a combination.

God, Paul taught, had humbled himself and come to earth in human form. Paul was the first to dwell on Jesus's dual nature—which later would become triple when the concept of the Holy Spirit was added to that nature.

Paul emphasized that Jesus had risen from the tomb, not as a spirit, but as living flesh. So, too, he taught, would those who believed in Jesus. Almost as important as the emphasis on life after death was his teaching that salvation—this bodily resurrection—could not be ensured simply by leading a moral life. Faith, he said, was what had "delivered us from the dominion of darkness and transferred us to the kingdom of his beloved Son" (Colossians 1:13–14). This was an important break with Judaism with its emphasis on keeping the law.

Predestination

But salvation, according to Paul, is open not to everyone but only to those who "are called according to his [God's] purpose." This idea of predestination—that God has preselected those to receive his grace—would echo through the centuries and become a controversial belief held by many Christians.

The idea of "God's elect" was not new. The Jews, in fact, considered

Architect of Christianity

Paul of Tarsus has been called the architect of Christianity who took the basic elements of the faith—the message of Jesus—and formed them into a religion. This summary of Paul's influence on Christianity is from Rev. James M. Stalker's The Life of St. Paul, *found on www.tks.org:*

"There are some men whose lives it is impossible to study without receiving the impression that they were expressly sent into the world to do a work required by the juncture of history on which they fell. . . . This impression is produced by no life more than by that of the apostle Paul. He was given to Christianity when it was in its most rudimentary beginnings. It was not indeed feeble. . . . But if we recognize that God makes use of means which commend themselves even to our eyes as suited to the ends he has in view, then we must say that the Christian movement at the moment when Paul appeared upon the stage was in the utmost need of a man of extraordinary endowments, who, becoming possessed with its genius, should incorporate it with the general history of the world; and in Paul it found the man it needed."

Paul of Tarsus molded Jesus's message into a religion.

themselves as the people chosen by God to keep the law. Paul, however, said that Jesus's love was universal, writing in Galatians (3:28), "There is neither Jew nor Greek, there is neither slave nor free, there is neither male nor female; for you are all one in Christ Jesus." Symbolic of how far Christianity had moved from Judaism was Paul's use of the Greek word for anointed, *christos*, rather than the Hebrew *messiah*.

Paul shaped Christianity in other basic ways. In addition to substituting *Christ* for *messiah*, he used the Greek *Jesus* instead of the Hebrew

Jeshua. He put great emphasis on the religious nature of the communal supper eaten by early Christian congregations, specifically likening it to the meal Jesus ate with his disciples on the night of his arrest.

His was the earliest version of the Last Supper of Jesus and the disciples, predating that of his companion Luke. In his first letter to the Corinthians (11:26) he told them, "For as often as you eat this bread and drink the cup, you proclaim the Lord's death until he comes." By emphasizing the importance of the Eucharist, as the communal meal taken on Sundays came to be called, from the Greek word for "giving thanks," Paul helped establish this first day of the week as the Christians' holy day, instead of Saturday, the Jewish Sabbath.

It is very likely that because of Paul's work among the Gentiles that Christianity survived. The church in Jerusalem remained small, unable to attract many converts from among the Jews. Many of the apostles were forced to flee from the wrath of Jewish officials and the Christian leader, James the Greater, was killed. Then, after a Jewish uprising in A.D. 68, the Roman emperor Vespian ordered his legions to destroy Jerusalem. The Christians, fearing the Romans would kill them all as they had killed Jesus, fled, effectively ending Christianity in Judea.

Paul's Death

Paul did not survive to see this happen. He had been attacked by a mob in Jerusalem in A.D. 58, and soldiers had to arrest him to prevent him from being lynched. As a Roman citizen, he asked for, and was granted, a trial in Rome. He was still a prisoner there in A.D. 64 when the emperor Nero, having blamed the Christians for a disastrous fire, vowed to wipe them out. According to tradition, Paul was executed on Nero's orders.

Christianity had entered a period of persecution that would last more than two and a half centuries, yet it not only would endure but would spread throughout the Roman Empire and begin to take on some of the form it would retain for almost two millennia. Eventually, though, one man's vision would turn a persecuted sect into the most powerful religion in the known world.

chapter | three

Persecution to Prominence

Although Christianity had spread far beyond the boundaries of Palestine, its survival was by no means ensured. The new religion had grown to the point where it attracted the attention, and the opposition, of both secular and religious authorities. Yet after centuries of persecution, Christianity would be lifted—traditionally, by a miracle— to a position of power and prominence.

The Romans' persecution of Christians was nowhere as constant and pervasive as is sometimes believed. Other than sporadic, isolated outbreaks, only five more emperors after Nero unleashed their fury against Christianity— Domitian in A.D. 89, Marcus Aurelius in 170, Decius in 249, Valerian in 253, and Diocletian in 303.

While they lasted, however, the persecutions had a curious dual effect. On one hand, they threatened to extinguish Christianity. Thousands met their deaths in the most gruesome manners their tormentors could devise—they were burned alive, torn apart by wild beasts, crucified, and boiled in oil. Some fled into the wilderness and starved; others were sold into slavery. Many succumbed to fear and renounced their faith.

On the other hand, however, the persecutions strengthened Christianity. For the most part, those who died did so with the greatest bravery, and their strength in the

A seventeenth-century Italian painting shows soldiers of King Herod slaying Jewish children. These children have been called the first Christian martyrs.

face of cruelty both bolstered the faith of the survivors and drew the admiration of onlookers. Just before his own execution in 165, Justin Martyr wrote, "We are beheaded, we are crucified, thrown to wild beasts, burned and put to every kind of torture. Everyone sees it. But, the more all this happens, the more numerous become those who believe through Jesus."[7] And the early Christian theologian Tertullian wrote, "The blood of the martyrs is seed [of the church]."[8] Those who gave their lives were accorded *sanctus*, or holy, status and were known as saints.

The Third Race

Rome was generally liberal toward established religions other than its own, and Christians were largely safe so long as the Romans thought Christianity was part of Judaism. Gradually, however, it became clear to the Romans that Christians did not obey Jewish law or follow Jewish practices. They came to be called the "third race"—neither Jewish nor pagan. Christianity became one of the unlicensed, or illicit, religions and therefore unprotected by law.

Christians were also held to be guilty of, in the words of the Roman historian Tacitus, "hatred of humankind."[9] This was because they refused to participate in public festivals and lived in groups apart from their fellow citizens. Furthermore, the secrecy in which they conducted their worship gave rise to wild rumors. Since they professed love among those they called "brothers and sisters," they were accused of incest. Since they supposedly ate someone's body and drank someone's blood, they were accused of cannibalism and sacrificing infants.

Both despite and because of the persecutions, however, Christianity continued to grow, helped in large measure by the Roman Empire itself. During the centuries of the *pax romana*, or Roman peace, borders were open to missionaries such as Paul, and Christians were generally free to preach in the marketplaces of cities they visited.

Not of This World

About A.D. 130, a man named Mathetes, about whom nothing more is known, wrote to an acquaintance named Diognetus. In it, he commuted on how Christians, while still carrying on day-to-day lives, seemed to also exist in a world of their own. This excerpt of the lengthy letter is found at www.earlychristianwritings.com:

"For Christians are not distinguished from the rest of mankind either in locality or in speech or in customs. For they dwell not somewhere in cities of their own, neither do they use some different language, nor practise an extraordinary kind of life. Nor again do they possess any invention discovered by any intelligence or study of ingenious men, nor are they masters of any human dogma as some are. But while they dwell in cities of Greeks and barbarians as the lot of each is cast, and follow the native customs in dress and food and the other arrangements of life, yet the constitution of their own citizenship, which they set forth, is marvellous, and confessedly contradicts expectation. They dwell in their own countries, but only as sojourners; they bear their share in all things as citizens, and they endure all hardships as strangers. Every foreign country is a fatherland to them, and every fatherland is foreign."

In the years between the persecutions, Christianity grew from a tiny offshoot of Judaism into a separate religion whose adherents could be found in every corner of the Roman Empire. It had particular appeal to the poorer classes—of which there were many—because it held out hope for a better afterlife. Gradually, however, it began to catch on among the more well-to-do, who, finding little fulfilling in pagan gods, were attracted by Christianity's dual message of love and ethical conduct.

Early Organization

As Christianity grew, better organization became necessary. A system of clergy evolved whereby men, but not women, could progress from a deacon, who might be in charge of funds or charitable works, to a presbyter or priest, who would preside at worship. When a congregation was exceptionally large or when a city held more than one church, a priest might be elected a bishop. A bishop was considered the heir of the original apostles, or disciples, and three other bishops had to agree to his election before he was consecrated. Bishops had considerable authority and were called "father"—*papa* or *pope* in Latin—although the exclusive use of the title by the bishop of Rome would not come into use until the 800s.

Church writings also became more organized; that is, the church determined which scriptures would be counted as being official and divinely inspired. The Jewish Torah —the first five books of what is now called the Old Testament—were accepted, as were the books relating to Jewish history, such as Judges and Kings. Also included were the writings of many prophets, including, naturally, Isaiah and others who predicted the coming of a messiah.

Of the many gospels—that is, accounts of Jesus's ministry that were thought to be written by those who knew him—four were chosen as being most authentic: Matthew, Mark, Luke, and John. Some of the more fanciful accounts, such as those supposedly written by the apostle Thomas, who had Jesus fashioning birds of clay and bringing them to life, were rejected.

Completing the New Testament were the epistles of Paul, those of James, Peter, John, and Jude, and the book of Revelations, the mysterious allegory written about A.D. 100 during the persecution by Domitian. Various churches, however, included or excluded books, and it was not until the 300s that the New Testament was fixed at twenty-seven books.

Nurtured by such visionaries as Paul, Christianity had prospered in the three centuries after Jesus's crucifixion, but it was still only one of many religions in the Roman Empire. Its survival was still in question, as evidenced by Diocletian's persecution when, according to Arthur James Mason, author of *The Persecutions of Diocletian*:

> the fiendish cruelty of Nero, the jealous fears of Domitian, the unimpassioned dislike of Marcus [Aurelius], the sweeping purpose of Decius, the clever devices of Valerian, fell into obscurity when compared with the concentrated terrors of that final grapple, which resulted in the destruction of the old Roman Empire and the establishment of the Cross as the symbol of the world's hope.[10]

Constantine

The man who brought about this great change may not even have been a Christian. Yet the Roman emperor Constantine, who accepted baptism only on his deathbed, had almost as great an impact on Christianity as Paul, starting in motion a series of fundamental changes.

In 293 a reorganization of the empire called for emperors and subemperors in the east and west. Instead of efficiency, however, the division of power led to civil war. In 306 the western emperor died and his son, Constantine, set out to rule the entire empire. He began his campaign in 312, massing his troops in Gaul (modern France) and marching across the Alps into Italy to face one of his rivals.

As Constantine approached Rome from the north, something happened that would forever change the history of Christianity. There are two accounts, both by Christian chroniclers who knew Constantine. Lactantius wrote that a voice told Constantine in a dream to place the Greek letters chi and rho on his soldiers' shields, these being the first two letters in the Greek word *christos*. Eusebius added that the emperor had seen a vision of a cross on the sun with the words *in hoc signo vinces*, or "conquer by this sign." At any rate, Constantine's troops—their shield emblazoned with the chi-rho symbol—were victorious at the decisive battle of Milvan Bridge.

Whatever Constantine had experienced prior to the battle, his victory convinced him of the power of the Christian God. Christian writers afterward explained that God had chosen Constantine just as he had chosen Paul. Certainly Constantine

The Conversion of Constantine

One of the most dramatic and momentous events in the history of Christianity occurred when the future emperor Constantine saw a vision. Using it as a guide, he won a crucial battle. The early Christian historian Eusebius of Caesarea knew Constantine and got the account from him firsthand. This excerpt from Eusebius is found at www.fordham.edu:

"He said that about noon . . . he saw with his own eyes the trophy of a cross of light in the heavens, above the sun, and bearing the inscription, CONQUER BY THIS. At this sight he himself was struck with amazement, and his whole army also, which followed him on this expedition, and witnessed the miracle.

"He said, moreover, that he doubted within himself what the import of this apparition could be. And while he continued to ponder and reason on its meaning, night suddenly came on; then in his sleep the Christ of God appeared to him with the same sign which he had seen in the heavens, and commanded him to make a likeness of that sign which he had seen in the heavens, and to use it as a safeguard in all engagements with his enemies.

"At dawn of day he arose, and communicated the marvel to his friends: and then, calling together the workers in gold and precious stones, he sat in the midst of them, and described to them the figure of the sign he had seen, bidding them represent it in gold and precious stones. And this representation I myself have had an opportunity of seeing."

could not have been looking for help from the Christians themselves, who were generally poor, powerless, and pacifist and made up only about a tenth of the population, but from this time forward, Christianity had a powerful friend.

The Edict of Milan

Constantine next formed an alliance with one of his remaining rivals, Licinius. They met at the Italian city of Milan in 313 to try to reach a political agreement. They issued the Edict of Milan, which, among other things, proclaimed religious tolerance throughout the empire: "It is one thing to enter voluntarily upon the struggle for immortality, another to compel others to do so from fear of punishment. . . . No person shall molest another; everyone shall keep in check the dictates of his heart . . . no one may, through his convictions, do harm to another."[11]

Constantine and Licinius were still in Milan when word came that a third claimant to the throne, Maximinus, had invaded Licinius's territory. Licinius mobilized his army and defeated Maximinus, who thereafter committed suicide. Constantine then bided his time, gathering his strength before attacking Licinius in 322. Two years later, Licinius was forced to abdicate, leaving Constantine master of the entire Roman Empire.

The new Roman emperor, however, had no fondness for the city of Rome itself. It was a stronghold of paganism, and the aristocrats who made up the senate considered Constantine something of an upstart. So in 330 Constantine capped his conquests by building a brilliant new capital well to the east at the ancient town of Byzantium on the strait that separates the Mediterranean and Black seas at the strategic junction of Europe and Asia. The new city was named for its founder—Constantinople.

Constantine felt he owed the defeat of his rivals to the Christian God. Furthermore, he desired to restore the glory of the empire as it had been at the time of Jesus's birth under the Emperor Augustus. Constantine believed this revitalized empire should have a central, unifying moral base and that Christianity was best suited to this purpose.

Imperial Favors

In favoring Christianity, Constantine did not attempt to end paganism. It was still far too strong, especially in rural areas. He did, however, make Christianity the beneficiary of many imperial favors. He decreed the return of all property confiscated from Christians during the persecutions. Christian priests and bishops were exempted from public service and the expenses thereby incurred. Some received direct cash payments. Laws enabled people to leave money and property to the church in their wills. Sunday, the Christians' holy day, was made an official day of rest. Constantine built Christian churches, including the massive St. Peter's in Rome above the spot where tradition said Peter was buried.

The man who did all this for Christianity was not himself a Christian. Most of his subjects were still pagan and Constantine took care to maintain good relations with them. Constantine's speeches show that he was a religious man who believed that "the holy service in which these hands have been busied has

An Italian Renaissance painting depicts Constantinople, founded by the Emperor Constantine in A.D. 330. The city became Christianity's center after Rome's decline.

begun in pure truth and faith toward God."[12] Yet he identified himself closely with the sun god Apollo, whose likeness appeared on the empire's coins. His benevolence toward Christians likely stemmed more from superstition than from faith. As a modern theologian puts it:

> For him [Constantine], the Christian God was a very powerful being who would support him as long as he favored the faithful. Therefore, when Constantine enacted laws in favor of Christianity,

and when he had churches built, what he sought was not the goodwill of Christians, but rather the goodwill of their God.[13]

Even Christians who had prayed for miraculous delivery from oppression could hardly believe the extent to which their prayers seemingly had been answered. Eusebius, a bishop of the time and the first historian of Christianity, wrote:

> All fear therefore of those who had formerly afflicted them was taken away from men, and they

celebrated splendid and festive days. Everything was filled with light, and those who before were downcast beheld each other with smiling faces and beaming eyes. With dances and hymns, in city and country, they glorified first of all God the universal King, because they had been thus taught, and then the pious emperor with his God-beloved children.[14]

Changes in Worship

Freed from persecution and enriched by Constantine's benevolence, Chris-tianity now quickly moved beyond its humble beginnings. Converts flocked to the church, many perhaps with an eye toward gaining favor rather than out of faith. To accommodate larger numbers, worship that had taken place for the most part in private homes now required large buildings. The early church buildings followed the pattern of the Roman basilica, or law court. The judge's chair became the bishop's throne. The altar to Minerva, the pagan goddess of wisdom, became the Christian altar. The entire area containing the

Origin of a Word

Many Christian words and terms have interesting derivations, but none more so than the word *chapel*, used to describe a small place of worship. The story of the word's origin dates from the 300s and involves Martin of Tours, who was a soldier before becoming a Christian and ultimately a saint.

The story goes that Martin and some companions were entering the city of Amiens in France on a very cold night when they were approached by a shivering beggar. Martin had no money but cut his soldier's cape in two and gave one half to the man to keep him warm.

That night in a dream, Martin saw Jesus, who spoke to him the quotation from Matthew (25:40), "Truly, I say to you, as you did it to one of the least of these my brethren, you did it to me."

What tradition says was a piece of Martin's cape was preserved in a small church. From the Latin word for cape, the church became known as the *cappella*, and the word was eventually applied to many small churches or smaller places of worship within very large churches. In English, of course, we know them as chapels and those who serve in them as chaplains.

clergy was called the chancel, from *cancelli*, a low divider that in the law court separated the judge and his assistants from the public.

Services became longer and more elaborate and showed a Roman influence. Clergy, especially bishops, began wearing costly robes and vestments. Incense, commonly used in pagan temples, was included in the service. Music grew in importance, and a section of the church was set aside in front of the chancel for the choir. What had been a simple, communal worship service was rapidly becoming a pageant in which ordinary believers played little part.

Church organization also took on more of a Roman flavor. Dioceses, areas under bishops' control, were grouped into provinces, each headed by an archbishop who was usually housed in the capital city of the imperial province. Clergy in these upper echelons grew wealthy from gifts and were among the emperor's closest advisers.

Monasticism

Many Christians were dismayed at what they considered a radical departure from Jesus's simple message of faith and love. It was impossible to find Jesus, they thought, amidst all the pomp and splendor. Their reac-

tion was to begin the movement that came to be known as monasticism, whereby individuals would practice physical self-denial in order to gain spiritual insight. Christian ascetics took their cue from Jesus, who the Bible says spent forty days and nights fasting in the desert. They withdrew from the world, living alone in caves or even atop pillars or in trees, gradually becoming known as monks, from the Greek word *monachos*, meaning "solitary." In addition, some who considered solitude insufficient ate barely enough to stay alive or punished their bodies in other ways.

When more and more people sought to escape the increasingly worldly church and learn a simpler form of Christianity, the solitary monk gave way to monastic communities. The founder of the first known Christian monastery was Pachomius, a Roman soldier and former pagan who around 325 retreated to the Egyptian desert, drew some scattered hermits together, and constructed a daily regimen of work, prayer, and meditation. He eventually founded eleven monasteries, and his sister Mary founded similar communities for women whose later counterparts would become known as nuns.

While the monks who followed Pachomius's strict rule had with-

Benedict is shown with some of his monks in this sixteenth-century Italian painting. The founder of the Benedictines emphasized learning as well as prayer in his order.

drawn from the world, even though in groups instead of alone, those organized around 358 by Basil added charity to their daily lives. After all, he taught, Jesus had returned from the desert to work among people. His monks, therefore, cared for the sick and established hospitals and orphanages.

The Benedictines

Monasteries did not appear in the western part of the Roman Empire until much later. The great innova-tor was Benedict of Nursia, who—in addition to prayer, meditation, and charitable work—made scholarship a monastic pursuit. Monks were required to study two hours a day, and many were put to work copying sacred texts and classical works.

Despite—or possibly because of —the strictness of the various rules, or prescribed regulations for daily life and worship, monasticism had great appeal to Christians. Martyrs who gave their lives for the church were replaced as heroes in people's eyes by monks and nuns, who gave their lives to the church. Those who entered monasteries or convents won great respect by so doing, and families frequently expressed gratitude to God by giving him one of their children to be raised as a monk or nun.

Monasticism was crucial to the development of Christianity. Until the rise of universities in the twelfth century, monasteries were the only seats of learning. Monks preserved both past and current knowledge, painstakingly copying religious and philosophical texts and frequently keeping them safe from the ravages of war. The Benedictine monks did much to preserve learning in the West after the fall of Rome. Likewise, monks in Ireland, which would remain largely untouched by European conflicts, kept some of the classical works of Greek philosophers from being lost forever.

Preservation of knowledge was only one facet of monasticism. Creation of knowledge was just as important. The quiet, contempla-

Monastic Rule

One of the great figures of the monastic movement within Christianity was Saint Benedict, who founded the Benedictine Order shortly after A.D. 500. Virtually every aspect of daily life and the Benedictine monks was laid down by The Rule of St. Benedict, *consisting of seventy-three chapters. This chapter, number 33, addresses the question of whether monks ought to have any possessions of their own. It is found at www.osb.org:*

"This vice [individual possessions] especially is to be cut out of the monastery by the roots. Let no one presume to give or receive anything without the Abbot's leave, or to have anything as his own—anything whatever, whether book or tablets or pen or whatever it may be—since they are not permitted to have even their bodies or wills at their own disposal; but for all their necessities let them look to the Father of the monastery. And let it be unlawful to have anything which the Abbot has not given or allowed. Let all things be common to all, as it is written (Acts 4:32), and let no one say or assume that anything is his own.

"But if anyone is caught indulging in this most wicked vice, let him be admonished once and a second time. If he fails to amend, let him undergo punishment."

tive life of monasteries provided an environment in which some of the most influential Christian thinking would be transferred to paper to thus be expounded to others.

The Monastic Schools

Along with preservation and creation, monasticism was largely responsible for the transfer of knowledge. Especially in the West, what little learning laypeople had, they had as a result of schools established by monasteries or convents. Wealthy people with some appreciation of learning sent their sons—and sometimes even their daughters—to such schools, and the religious houses were the only recourse for anyone who possessed a keen intellect and the desire to develop it.

The transfer of knowledge also involved missionary work. In later centuries, when barbarian tribes threatened to extinguish Christianity in northern Europe, monks, particularly those from Ireland, would carry the faith to those areas in which it might otherwise be lost and to other areas in which it had never existed.

Christianity had now become firmly established as the primary religion in the Roman Empire. Exactly what shape that religion would take became less clear as internal differences began to appear in the church. These disagreements over both doctrine and practice would begin the process of dividing and subdividing Christianity that has continued to the present day.

chapter four

Heresy and Schism

When Christianity reached its new status under Constantine, it no longer had to battle for survival by defending its beliefs against pagans. This did not eliminate conflict, however, as Christians began to battle among themselves over what it was they should believe. This conflict was not at all what Constantine wanted in a religion that was supposed to bind his empire together and was what Paul had warned the Ephesians against (4:5) when he called for "one Lord, one faith, one baptism."

Both Constantine and Paul had thought that the strength of the church depended on orthodoxy, a strict set of beliefs from which there could be no departure. Only a universal adherence to one set of beliefs, the orthodox contended, would find favor with God. Indeed, by the end of the second century, Orthodox Christians were referring to their church as Catholic, from the Greek word for "universal."

Departures from orthodoxy were considered heresy and were nothing new for Christianity, even in Constantine's time. The Gnostics, for instance, believed (among other things) that a person's body is inherently evil. Therefore, according to their beliefs, even though Jesus resembled a man outwardly, he could not have been in any way human.

This was heresy to Christians who held the orthodox belief that Jesus was both human and divine. The church reacted around A.D. 150 by requiring new members to swear their belief in a series of three statements later known as the Apostles' Creed, which is still recited in many churches. In reciting the creed, the newly minted Christians swore that they believed, first, in God; second, in Jesus Christ; and third, in the Holy Spirit, the church, and in resurrection after death. The second statement concerning Jesus was very specific, identifying him as the son of God, who was born to a human mother and who lived, died, and rose from the dead.

The Trinity

The Apostles' Creed was built around the concept of God as three aspects—God, Jesus, and Holy Spirit. This concept was rooted in Matthew's Gospel (28:19) in which Jesus told the apostles to "go therefore and make disciples of all nations, baptizing them in the name of the Father

The part of the Trinity known as the Holy Spirit is frequently pictured as a descending dove, as in this sixteenth-century Italian painting.

and of the Son and of the Holy Spirit." One early theologian, Tertullian, explained this Holy Trinity by writing that God exists in three persons but is also one person made up of three substances. There were plenty of alternate theories about God's nature, however, and seemingly everyone embracing a particular theory believed everyone else not only to be misguided but also to be guilty of heresy. Christianity's great schisms, or divisions, in the centuries immediately after Constantine would involve the relationships of the three parts of the Holy Trinity.

The most widespread and divisive heresy—yet so persuasive that it continues—was Arianism. Arius, a priest in the Egyptian city of Alexandria, taught that the Father and Son were not together eternal nor of the same substance. Jesus, Arius said, was not equal to God as part of the Trinity but was a creation of God and therefore not divine.

Such views could not be tolerated by Alexander, bishop of Alexandria, who excommunicated Arius in 320 and exiled him to Illyria, an area that encompasses present-day Albania and Bosnia. From there, Arius wrote letters of protest to other influential bishops, convincing some that he was correct. His followers stirred up the people of Alexandria, who marched through the streets, shouting, "There was [a time] when he [Jesus] was not."[15]

Theological argument was not something engaged in only by the clergy. Ordinary people followed the debate with lively interest and did not hesitate to do some debating of their own. "If you ask someone to give you change, he philosophizes about the Begotten and Unbegotten," one bishop grumbled. "If you say to the attendant, 'Is my bath ready?' he tells you that the Son was made out of nothing."[16]

Such doctrinal squabbling was not at all to Constantine's liking. He wrote to the warring factions, "O most merciful providence of God, what a wound did my ears receive when I learned that you were contending about mere words, points difficult to understand, and unprofitable in any case—squabbles, the fruit of misused leisure."[17]

The Council of Nicea

Constantine first sent Bishop Hosius of Spain to mediate the dispute, but Hosius had to report to his master that reconciliation of the two views was impossible. The emperor then called in 325 the first of the great ecumenical, or universal, councils in the city of Nicea in northern Turkey and presided over it himself.

The Council of Nicea

The first great meeting of worldwide Christianity—or at least as much of the world as Christianity covered in A.D. 325—was the Council of Nicea. It was called by Emperor Constantine in an effort to prevent the so-called Arian Heresy from tearing the church in two.

Eusebius of Caesarea, in his Life of Constantine, *described the scene, as found in* The Story of Christianity, *by Justo L. González:*

"There were gathered the most distinguished ministers of God, from the many churches in Europe, Libya [i.e., Africa] and Asia. A single house of prayer, as if enlarged by God, sheltered Syrians and Cilicians, Phoenicians and Arabs, delegates from Palestine and from Egypt, Thebans and Libyans, together with those from Mesopotamia. Thee was also a Persian bishop, and a Scythian was not lacking. Pontius, Galatia, Pamphylia, Cappodocia, Asia, and Phrygia sent their most outstanding bishops, jointly with those from the remotest areas of Thrace, Macedonia, Achaia, and Epirus. Even from Spain, there was a man of great fame who sat as a member of the great assembly. The bishop of the Imperial City [Rome] could not attend due to his advanced age; but he was represented by his presbyters. Constantine is the first ruler of all time to have gathered such a garland in the bond of peace and to have presented it to his Savior as an offering of gratitude for the victories he had won over all his enemies."

More than three hundred bishops attended the council, most of them from the Greek-speaking eastern part of the empire. Partly because of the emperor's decision to locate his capital in the east, the church in the Latin-speaking west had relatively little influence under Constantine. The bishop of Rome, at this time only one of many bishops called pope, was so uninterested that he did not attend but sent two priests as representatives. Nevertheless, it was a magnificent mo-ment for Christianity as churchmen from throughout the known world, some of them bearing the scars of earlier persecution, met in splendor.

When the anti-Arians tried to support their views with quotations of scripture, they ran into difficulties. The Arians could muster just as many citations on their side, such as John 17:3, which implies that Jesus was not God but God's appointed messenger. Still, opponents of Arius dominated the council from the outset. The majority of

This Italian fresco shows the Council of Nicea, convened in A.D. 325. A primary result of the council was the Nicene Creed, a basic statement of Christian beliefs.

bishops countered Arianism the same way the church had previously countered Gnosticism: by fashioning a creed that would set forth basic Christian belief.

This Nicene Creed followed the same general pattern as the Apostles' Creed, but Jesus was pointedly described as "begotten of the Father, Only-begotten, That is, of one substance with the Father."[18] Controversy over the wording continued. Three subsequent councils tried to reach a compromise, but finally the original wording was restored in 381 at a council in Constantinople.

Monophysites and Dyophysites

Arians refused to give in. In about 445, a monk named Eutyches began to preach that, while Jesus was "of one substance" with God, he was not of one substance with humanity —that he had become wholly divine after his birth. The church rapidly split into two camps: The followers of Eutyches were called monophysites—"one nature"—and their opponents dyophysites— "dual nature." Another council, this one at Chalcedon near Constantinople in 451, decided the issue in favor of the dyophysites.

The monophysites persisted and formed strongholds in Egypt, Ethiopia, Armenia, and Syria. The Christian churches in those areas would cling to a belief in the single nature of Jesus into the twenty-first century.

Christianity was now the official religion of the Roman Empire, having been so designated in 391 by Emperor Theodosius, who banned all pagan worship. The church had settled on the Trinity and on the nature of Jesus—at least for the time being —but still the unity of the church had been shattered to the point where the monastic founder Basil compared it to a "tattered old coat."[19]

These endless controversies served to widen the gulf between East and West begun when Diocletian divided the empire in 286. Underlying the divergence were differing cultural viewpoints. Christianity in the East tended to reflect the mysticism common to other religions practiced in the area, such as Zoroastrianism in Persia and the Egyptian worship of Isis and Osiris. Westerners, with their long tradition of Roman law, took a more practical view. The East sought to find what Christianity was. The West sought to find how it worked.

Papal Power

Increasingly, however, the division between East and West was more about who ran the church than what Christianity was. In Rome the popes were increasing their prestige and authority. In particular, the bishops of Rome had long asserted that they were in a direct line of succession from Peter. Furthermore, they claimed, Jesus had told Peter (Matthew 16:19) that "whatever you bind on earth shall be bound in heaven, and whatever you loose on earth shall be loosed in heaven."

Leo I, pope from 440 to 461, took this to mean that whoever was bishop of Rome should have supreme authority over all of Christianity. Naturally, the patriarchs—the heads of the major churches in the East— denied owing any obedience to Rome, even though they acknowledged its seniority.

Eastern leaders also resented the popes' inserting themselves in what were essentially Eastern theological questions. Leo, for instance, had been instrumental in the convening of the Council of Chalcedon, and although he did not attend in person, his representatives presented his views, which formed the basis for the council's affirmation of the dyophysites' assertion of Jesus's dual nature.

The issue of Jesus's nature, however, continued to plague the East. Despite the decision at Chalcedon, Alexandria continued as a monophysite stronghold. Refugees went to Egypt to flee persecution by the dyophysite majority. Syria also was solidly in the monophysite camp, and the quarrel threatened to split the Eastern Empire.

Justinian

The empire unified by Constantine was again divided into East and West in 395, and the Western Empire came to an end in 476 as the result of a long series of invasions by Germanic tribes. In 527, however, the most able emperor of the east, Justinian, came to power and

The Pope and the Barbarian

In 453 Attila the Hun led his hordes into Italy and threatened to overrun Rome. Civil authority would do nothing, so it was up to the pope, Leo I, to try to save the city. An anonymous chronicler gave this account of the meeting. It is found in the Internet Medieval Source Book, *edited by Paul Halsall, and found at www.fordham.edu:*

"He [Leo] met Attila, it is said, in the neighborhood of the river Mincio, and he spoke to the grim monarch, saying 'The senate and the people of Rome, once conquerors of the world, now indeed vanquished, come before thee as suppliants. We pray for mercy and deliverance. Thou hast subdued, O Attila, the whole circle of the lands which it was granted to the Romans, victors over all peoples, to conquer. Now we pray that thou, who hast conquered others, shouldst conquer thyself. The people have felt thy scourge; now as suppliants they would feel thy mercy.' As Leo said these things Attila stood looking upon his venerable garb and aspect, silent, as if thinking deeply. And lo, suddenly there were seen the apostles Peter and Paul, clad like bishops, standing by Leo, the one on the right hand, the other on the left. They held swords stretched out over his head, and threatened Attila with death if he did not obey the pope's command. Wherefore Attila was appeased. . . . He by Leo's intercession, straightway promised a lasting peace and withdrew beyond the Danube."

Pope Leo I meets Attila the Hun outside Rome in this Italian painting. By convincing Attila not to attack the city, Leo greatly increased the prestige of the papacy.

in 533 set out to reconquer the parts of the West. Barely ten years later his armies had taken North Africa, Spain, and Italy.

Justinian also sought a compromise between Orthodox Christians and the monophysites, partially to restore peace to the empire and partially due to the wishes of his empress, Theodora, a confirmed monophysite. His strategy was to issue an imperial edict confirming Chalcedon but condemning the writings of three theologians to whom the monophysites objected. When Pope Vigilius of Rome resisted, Justinian had him kidnapped and brought to Constantinople, where he was forced to yield.

Justinian's edict was upheld by the Council of Constantinople in 553, but his efforts at winning unity had failed. The monophysites still refused

Emperor and Church

The relationship between church and state was seldom closer, though not necessarily equitable, than in the Eastern Roman Empire. This summary is found in The Horizon History of Christianity, *by Roland Herbert Bainton:*

"'There are two main gifts bestowed by God upon men,' Justinian's code proclaimed, 'the priesthood and the imperial authority.' In theory, the two were equal, but in practice the Church was usually subordinate to the state, and emperors shuffled patriarchs about freely. But the patriarchs themselves were not

without power. Michael Cerularius, who headed the Church at the time of the break with Rome in 1054, adopted the habit of wearing purple sandals, symbol of imperial authority; at one time he told the emperor: 'I raised you up, you imbecile, but I'll break you.' As it happened, the emperor broke him, but other emperors were often less successful in controlling the Church, particularly when they were guilty of crimes for which the patriarchs demanded penance."

Justinian, like other emperors of the East, subordinated the church to the state.

to accept Jesus's dual nature, and bishops in the West were enraged by the emperor's handling of Vigilius, who died on his way back to Rome in 555. It would be nearly a century before church leaders, at a meeting known to history as the Lateran Synod, restored partial harmony.

Muhammad and Islam

Meanwhile, the Eastern Church had a far more serious problem on its hands, one that would change not only the face of Christianity and the Roman Empire but the entire world. Around 610 a young merchant in the Arab city of Mecca had a vision in which the archangel Gabriel told him he was the messenger of God. He gathered followers and founded a new religion, Islam.

Muhammad believed that he was called on to spread his beliefs, by conquest if necessary. By the time of his death in 632, the entire Arabian Peninsula had been united under Islam, which would sweep across much of the Eastern Empire. Damascus fell in 632, Jerusalem in 638, Alexandria in 642, and Carthage in 695. Muslim armies crossed the Straits of Gibraltar in 711 and conquered Spain. Only a defeat at the hands of the Franks under Charles Martel in 732 pre-vented them from conquering the rest of Europe.

The effect of the Islamic conquests on Christianity was enormous, especially in the East. Except for Constantinople, all the great centers of Eastern Christianity were lost—Alexandria, Antioch, Jerusalem, and the entire Holy Land. Blocked on the east and south, the Orthodox church expanded northwest into Bulgaria and north into Russia. This last expansion was most important. Centuries later, after what remained of the Byzantine Empire was swallowed up by Islam, the Russian Orthodox church would remain as the largest surviving segment of Eastern Christianity.

The Photian Schism

At the same time the Eastern Church was under pressure from Islam, it was embroiled in numerous

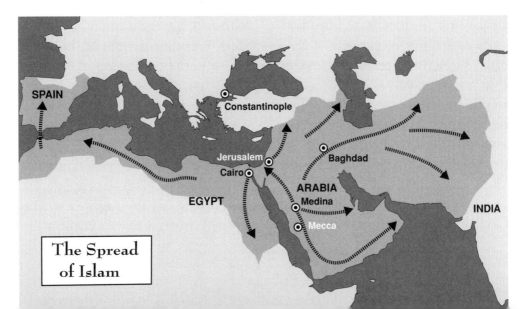

SPAIN

Constantinople

Jerusalem

Cairo

Baghdad

ARABIA

Medina

EGYPT

Mecca

INDIA

The Spread of Islam

feuds with the church in the West. In 858 a bitter controversy resulted in the election of rival patriarchs of Constantinople—Ignatius and Photius. Both turned to Pope Nicholas I, who gave his support to Ignatius.

Photius promptly declared that the entire Catholic Church was ridden with heresy. First, he said, the Western ban on married clergy, although not strictly enforced, was not supported by scripture. Second, the West used for Communion bread that was unleavened, or without yeast, rather than the leavened variety used in the East.

Most important, Photius said, the Catholics had unilaterally altered the Nicene Creed, saying the Holy Spirit proceeds "from the Father and the Son" rather than "from the Father." Orthodox clergy were outraged, and Photius called a council in 867 that excommunicated the pope.

The quarrels over these differences were eventually patched up, but both sides remained suspicious of each other. Underlying relations between East and West was tension over who should lead Christendom. The East could not accept Rome's increasing assertion that the pope had authority over the entire church, while the West could not accept Constantinople's focus on the emperor as God's earthly representative.

Events reached a breaking point in 1054. The patriarch of Constantinople, Michael Cerularius, attempted to enforce religious uniformity throughout the empire. This included shutting down churches in the East that catered to Western visitors by using unleavened bread in Communion. The situation grew worse when a Bulgarian Orthodox bishop renewed the claims of heresy in the West over both unleavened bread and the prohibition of married clergy.

The Rash Cardinal

Pope Leo IX sent an ambassador to try to settle the differences, but the man he chose, Cardinal Humbert, was a zealot who abhorred Eastern practices, particularly married clergy and the authority of the emperor over the church. Instead of trying to negotiate, Humbert demanded that the Orthodox church acknowledge the supremacy of the pope. Cerularius refused, but that was only the beginning of a diplomatic spat that would have lasting consequences.

On June 6, 1054, as Cerularius was preparing to administer Communion in the great church of Saint Sophia, Humbert appeared, marched up to the high altar, and slapped down a document that, in the pope's name, excommunicated Cerularius as a heretic. Humbert then promptly returned to Rome.

Cerularius responded by convening a council that excommunicated the pope. This time there would be no smoothing over of differences. Any hope of reconciliation was shattered in 1204, when Catholic crusaders brutally sacked Constantinople. The split between Catholic and Orthodox Christianity was such that it remains unhealed eight hundred years later.

After the rival excommunications, the Western and Eastern churches went their separate ways. The Byzantine Empire would survive until 1453, when it fell to the Ottoman Turks, who permitted the Orthodox church to continue in what became an Islamic empire. Christianity had now become a mi-

nority, marginalized religion in the lands that had given it birth. Outside the Islamic world, Orthodox churches continued to prosper in Greece, Russia, Armenia, and in the Balkans, but the Orthodox church, writes contemporary historian Brian Moynahan, "lived off its inheritance. Its purpose was *agalma*, or 'statuesque calm,' and it lacked the restless dynamic that stamped the Western faith."[20]

After 1054, the focus of Christian growth and development was almost entirely in the West. Popes grew ever more powerful, rivaling kings in political power and creating a climate in which church and state would clash in a battle of wills. With power would also come corruption. The church grew more worldly, and—in the eyes of many—increasingly remote from the teachings of Jesus.

chapter | five

Power and Perversion

In John 10:16, Jesus envisioned Christianity as "one flock, one shepherd." That vision of unity, Paul's universal church, was shattered by the split between East and West. It seemed for a time that the Western Church, Roman Catholicism, would achieve such accord as the papacy grew ever more powerful. Along with great power, however, came its frequent companion, corruption, and the excesses of some medieval popes set the stage for still more discord and division.

From the late fifth century through the Middle Ages, the Roman Catholic Church based much of its claim to ultimate supremacy on Augustine, bishop of Hippo in North Africa from 391 to 430. The authority of the church was a prevalent theme in Augustine's writings, considered by historians second only to Paul in their impact on the Western Church. When some in the church proposed that people could achieve salvation through their own efforts, Augustine countered that humanity is inherently sinful and had been so since Adam and Eve disobeyed God in the Garden of Eden as told in the book of Genesis. Salvation, he said, comes only through God by way of the church. This doctrine, sometimes referred to as original sin, became a foundation later for those defending the church's authority.

One of Augustine's most influential works, *The City of God*, addressed something a good deal less philosophical than original sin. Rome, for centuries a symbol of strength and stability, had been sacked in 410 by Germanic invaders known as Visigoths. This was just one of many misfortunes that had befallen Christendom. Another Germanic tribe, the Vandals, had crossed the Rhine River in 407 and swept through France, Spain, and most of North Africa. Even though they had been converted to Christianity, the Vandals were monophysites and slaughtered Orthodox clergy without mercy.

Augustine's *City of God*

It was amid such calamities that Augustine wrote *The City of God*. Rome, he said, was destined to fall because all earthly empires are corrupted by a lust for power. Only the City of God, built on love, is eternal. God had used Rome for his purpose—the spread of Christianity—and then let it go the way of previous empires.

While Augustine maintained that the City of God is unattainable on earth, he did allow that it can be approached in a society where the church and state are inseparable and work in harmony—the state upholding and protecting the church and the church ensuring that the state acts in a moral manner. This concept of the intertwining of church and state would dominate western European thinking for more than a thousand years. Religious tolerance and deviations from orthodoxy were unthinkable, since an attack on the church was also an attack on the state.

Augustine added that only the moral state can legitimately engage in war and then only if it is fought against an unjust foe and if the objective is to bring about peace. This idea established a pattern for the future in which rulers would seek to justify armed conflict on the basis of the guilt or misdeeds of their foes, claiming that God was on their side.

Barbarian attacks continued, but despite (or possibly because of) these, Western Christianity slowly achieved the unity that had escaped the East. One by one the barbarians were won over to Christianity as it was practiced in the West. The Frankish king Clovis was baptized in 496. The king of the Burgundians converted in 516 and the Visigoth king Recared in 589.

These conversions further enmeshed the church in European politics. When the pagan tribes

Augustine on the Just Ruler

Augustine, in his The City of God, *said that Christians should make earthly cities as much like the City of God as possible. One way is for the people and church to support and obey the ruler and, at the same time, for the ruler to govern according to Christian values. This excerpt on how to rule others, from Book XIX, is found at http:ccat.sas. upenn.edu:*

"And this is the order of this concord, that a man, in the first place, injure no one, and, in the second, do good to every one he can reach. Primarily, therefore, his own household are his care, for the law of nature and of society gives him readier access to them and greater opportunity of serving them. And hence the apostle says, 'Now, if any provide not for his own, and specially for those of his own house, he hath denied the faith, and is worse than an infidel.' This is the origin of domestic peace, or the well-ordered concord of those in the family who rule and those who obey. . . . [In] the family of the just man who lives by faith and is as yet a pilgrim journeying on to the celestial city, even those who rule serve those whom they seem to command; for they rule not from a love of power, but from a sense of the duty they owe to others—not because they are proud of authority, but because they love mercy."

Augustine advocated partnership between church and state.

were converted, the usual pattern was for missionaries to convert the king. Once the king became a Christian, all his subjects did likewise. It was an extremely practical method, but it resulted in the church depending on the cooperation of earthly rulers.

Still, peace between the barbarians and what remained of the Western Roman Empire did not last. In 568 the Lombards, one of the tribes not yet converted to Christianity, invaded Italy. They were prevented from sacking Rome by Pope Pelagius II, but the city subsequently endured a series of attacks and sieges that reduced it to a shell of its former glory. The population fell from eight hundred thousand in 400 to about thirty thousand in 600. Buildings had been ransacked for stones to rebuild city walls. A flood in 589 ruined crops and spread disease.

Gregory I is considered the father of the modern papacy.

Gregory I

With no civil authority in evidence, it was up to the church and a remarkable pope—Gregory I—to bring order. Gregory had had no wish to be pope and had tried to avoid it. Once elected, however, he put his administrative and diplomatic genius to work. He directly negotiated peace with the Lombards. He supervised the rebuilding of Rome's aqueducts to ensure a water supply. He organized the distribution of food, much of it from estates owned by the papacy in Sicily and elsewhere. He became, in effect, the real ruler of Rome and the surrounding area.

Gregory reinforced the papacy's claim to authority over all Christianity, claiming it was the pope alone to whom "the care and principate [rule] of the whole Church was committed."[21] Rather than try to establish any authority in the East, however, Gregory concentrated on bringing more of the West under Rome. He strengthened the church in Gaul and used it for his greatest mission, the conversion of England.

Gregory was a firm disciple of Augustine and used many of Augustine's doctrines to substantiate his own views. He took the concept of a just war and used it to advocate force, if necessary, to convert unbelievers.

Purgatory

More important from a theological standpoint, Gregory advanced Augustine's idea that those who had received God's grace but who died in sin required a time of purification before entering heaven. This would lead to the doctrine of purgatory, from which the living can

help the dead escape by praying for them and making offerings in their name. Gregory also strengthened the concept that the living can gain God's forgiveness for sins through a process of penance, including the receiving of formal absolution from a priest.

When Gregory died in 604 he had laid the foundations for what the papacy would become in the Middle Ages: the supreme spiritual authority and a powerful political force throughout the West. The foundations would be strengthened two hundred years later when the church firmly allied itself with the strongest of the emerging European states.

Gregory's successors lacked his ability, and by the 700s, the papacy had become a battleground for powerful Italian families. In 799, after being savagely attacked in a Roman street by rivals, Pope Leo III took refuge with the strongest ruler in the West—Charlemagne, king of the Franks and ruler of much of Europe. Charlemagne marched into Rome, restored Leo to power, and on Christmas Day in 800 was crowned emperor by the pope.

Leo had inaugurated what would become known as the Holy Roman Empire. That is to say, by personally placing the crown on Char-

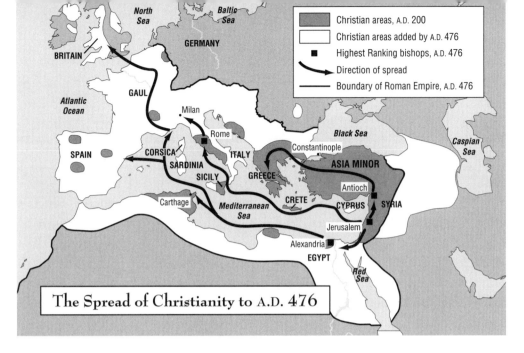

The Spread of Christianity to A.D. 476

lemagne, he also symbolically established the claim that the emperor—and, by extension, other earthly rulers—needed official sanction by the church. Scholars have debated whether or not Charlemagne knew beforehand that he would be crowned by the pope, and if so, whether he would have consented, thus diminishing his own stature.

Decline of the Papacy

Charlemagne's vast empire did not long outlive him, and as the empire declined, so did the papacy. Indeed, the ninth and tenth centuries saw some of the worst popes in history. Stephen VI, pope from 885 to 891, dug up the corpse of his predecessor and put it on trial. John XII, only a teenager when elected in 955,

was notorious for sexual escapades before he was finally strangled by an outraged husband. Unfortunately, Stephen and John were by no means exceptions to the rule.

This is not to say that the church was totally corrupt. Desire for reform and adherence to pious behavior found outlets in the monasteries. Cluny, founded in France in 909, spread its rule of piety to houses all over Europe. The Cluniacs, who were independent of secular rulers, preached against the naming of bishops and abbots by kings. They also practiced the rule of celibacy with such zeal that it became the norm over Europe.

Other monastic movements followed, such as the Cistercians in the 1100s. The two most influential orders, however, came early in the

61

1200s with the creation of the Franciscans and the Dominicans, who had two very different missions. The Franciscans followed the example of their founder, Francis of Assisi, who advocated a life of poverty, preaching, and service to others, especially to the poor and sick. The order founded by Dominic, on the other hand, was dedicated primarily to education, training its members to battle heresy and to undertake missionary work in the Islamic lands.

As significant as the contributions of these monasteries were, equally important to Christian thought were the scholastics. These thinkers were to be found in universities rather than monasteries. The scholastics, building on the works of the Greek philosopher Aristotle, recently reintroduced in the West, sought to examine religious questions from the standpoint of reason—that which can be proved or demonstrated—instead of through faith alone.

Thomas Aquinas

The greatest of the scholastics was Thomas Aquinas, who wrote in the mid-1200s. In works such as his *Summa Theologica*, or *Summary of Theology*, Thomas held that reason and faith are not mutually exclusive, but that both are gifts of God.

Human knowledge, he wrote, comes first from human senses—sound, sight, touch, and so on. Although he concedes that some universal truths are beyond reason and must rely on faith to be understood, others—such as the existence of God—can be reached through reason. Thomas's carefully constructed theological model was especially valuable since it found a way to give validity to both the knowable—Jesus's humanity and God's visible creation—and the unknowable—the essence of the human soul and God's will.

Thomas's thinking had much more influence centuries later than during his lifetime. In the seventeenth and eighteenth centuries it became the basis for the rationalist Christian viewpoints of philosophers such as René Descartes, David Hume, and Immanuel Kant. And in 1879 Pope Leo XII would declare Thomas's concepts to be the official theology of the Roman Catholic Church.

In the meantime, however, the chaotic state of church leadership continued until Emperor Henry III, in 1046, removed the sitting pope and installed his own choice, Pope Leo IX. The new pope undertook a vigorous program to end simony, the practice of purchasing appointments

Thomas Aquinas

One of philosopher Thomas Aquinas's most important teachings was that reason and faith are not mutually exclusive and can coexist within Christianity. This passage is from his Summa Contra Gentiles, *or* Summary Against the Gentiles. *It is found on www.nd.edu:*

"The natural dictates of reason must certainly be quite true: it is impossible to think of their being otherwise. Nor again is it permissible to believe that the tenets of faith are false, being so evidently confirmed by God. Since therefore falsehood alone is contrary to truth, it is impossible for the truth of faith to be contrary to principles known by natural reason.

"Whatever is put into the disciple's mind by the teacher is contained in the knowledge of the teacher, unless the teacher is teaching dishonestly, which would be a wicked thing to say of God. But the knowledge of principles naturally known is put into us by God, seeing that God Himself is the author of our nature. Therefore these principles also are contained in the Divine Wisdom. Whatever therefore is contrary to these principles is contrary to Divine Wisdom, and cannot be of God.

"Contrary reasons fetter our intellect fast, so that it cannot proceed to the knowledge of the truth. If therefore contrary informations were sent us by God, our intellect would be thereby hindered from knowledge of the truth: but such hindrance cannot be of God."

Thomas Aquinas taught that reason and faith could coexist within Christianity.

to church posts, but this created tension with some secular rulers who administered and benefited from selling clerical positions.

This tension came to a head during the reign of Pope Gregory VII. In 1075 Emperor Henry IV deposed some German bishops and appointed replacements. The pope, who declared that only he could appoint and install new bishops, demanded the emperor appear before him in Rome. Henry refused and Gregory responded by both excommunicating the emperor and declaring him deposed from his throne.

The Penitent King

Henry thought his bishops and people would support him. They did not, afraid that they, too, would

A humbled Emperor Henry IV stands before Pope Gregory VII to beg for forgiveness after being excommunicated.

Ultimate Papal Power

The ultimate expression of the power of the pope and the Roman Catholic Church was the papal bull "Unam Sanctam," (One Holy), issued by Pope Boniface VIII in 1302. This excerpt is found at www.fordham.edu:

"Hence we must recognize the more clearly that spiritual power surpasses in dignity and in nobility any temporal power whatever, as spiritual things surpass the temporal. This we see very clearly also by the payment, benediction, and consecration of the tithes, but the acceptance of power itself and by the government even of things. For with truth as our witness, it belongs to spiritual power to establish the terrestrial power and to pass judgment if it has not been good. . . . This authority, however, (though it has been given to man and is exercised by man), is not human but rather divine, granted to Peter by a divine word and reaffirmed to him (Peter) and his successors by the One Whom Peter confessed, the Lord saying to Peter himself, 'Whatsoever you shall bind on earth, shall be bound also in Heaven,' etc., [Matthew 16:19]. Therefore whoever resists this power thus ordained by God, resists the ordinance of God. . . . Furthermore, we declare, we proclaim, we define that it is absolutely necessary for salvation that every human creature be subject to the Roman Pontiff."

be excommunicated. In one of the most dramatic scenes in history, the emperor—barefoot and dressed only in a coarse robe—stood for three days in the snow outside the pope's castle. Gregory forgave the emperor, who promised to obey him.

Gregory's victory was short-lived. Henry consolidated his power and in 1084 invaded Italy, took Rome, and deposed Gregory in favor of his own candidate. Gregory died soon afterward, but his suc-cessors battled first with Henry, then with his son, Henry V, before a compromise on the question of who could make clerical appointments was reached.

Of great significance was the precedent Gregory had set by acting directly against a secular ruler. A few years later, Innocent III raised the papacy to heights never reached before or since. He dominated European politics, excommunicating and deposing kings—or threatening to do so—until his wishes were obeyed.

The Holy Roman Empire continued to pose the greatest threat to papal power, and Innocent and his successors sought to curb the power of the emperors by supporting their rivals, the increasingly powerful kings of France. This had the effect, however, of putting the papacy under the thumb of French kings. This situation reached a climax in 1302 when Pope Boniface VIII issued a bull, or proclamation, saying that "it is absolutely necessary for salvation that all human creatures be under the Roman pontiff."[22]

When King Philip IV of France refused to obey Boniface's decree, the pope prepared to excommunicate him. Before he could, however, French agents kidnapped Boniface and tried to force him to resign. He refused but died shortly thereafter. His successor, Benedict XII, reigned only one year before his sudden death, reportedly by poison. Then, in 1305, Philip had a French bishop elected pope.

The Babylonian Captivity

The new pope, Clement V, lived in France and never during his reign set foot in Rome. In 1309 he established a residence in the French city of Avignon, and a succession of French popes were to make it their headquarters until Gregory XI returned to Rome in 1377. This period in church history has become known as the Babylonian Captivity.

The return to Rome did not solve the papacy's problems. Over the next four or five decades, rivals for the papacy—two or even three at a time—bitterly fought each other. The spectacle of warring popes hurling excommunications at one another severely weakened the papacy's image in the eyes of Christian Europe.

Eventually what came to be called the Great Western Schism was settled, but this did little to restore its image. Indeed, many of the popes of the 1400s and early 1500s behaved every bit as scandalously as their predecessors four hundred years earlier. They cared little for religion, much preferring to wage war, collect art, and enrich their relatives, including, on occasion, their illegitimate children.

All such worldly pursuits cost money, and the popes of the fifteenth and early sixteenth centuries raised it by whatever means possible. Simony flourished. Noble families spent huge sums to make younger sons, some of them barely into their teens, bishops or cardinals. If one high office failed to bring in sufficient income, a person could hold more than one, a practice known as pluralism.

Indulgences

Nothing, however, angered would-be reformers more than indulgences. According to Roman Catholic doctrine, it is possible for someone who has committed a sin to go beyond confessing the sin and, through an act of repentance, be granted an indulgence. Indulgences are based in part on the idea that Jesus took the sins of humanity on himself and thus built up a treasury of forgiveness.

Sinners can draw on that treasury, if sanctioned by church authority, through prayer, fasting, or the giving of alms (donations to God). Such acts, in effect, pay a debt to God and lessen the time one's soul must spend in purgatory before sins

are wiped out and the soul may proceed to heaven.

Popes had used indulgences to raise money before, but nowhere near the scale used by Julius II. In 1513, when Julius needed money for rebuilding St. Peter's Basilica, agents of the pope went throughout Europe doing a brisk business. People were given the impression they could buy their way into heaven, even paying for sins yet to be committed, something clearly not supported by church teaching. They were also told they could buy indulgences to help speed to heaven the souls of loved ones already dead. Reform-minded clergy were outraged, no one more so than a German monk named Martin Luther, and his outrage began what is known as the Protestant Reformation.

chapter | six

Reformation and Counter-Reformation

The fabric of Christianity, which Paul had envisioned as a seamless garment covering the entire body of the church, had been ripped in two by the East-West schism. The excesses of the medieval popes then provoked a reaction that split Christianity even further—the Protestant Reformation.

The division between Catholic and Protestant, in turn, would lead to extreme brutality on both sides and even within factions of each side. The misery visited on Europe in the name of God and Jesus and the endless bickering over minute theological issues eventually ushered in the modern era, one in which the very value of religion came under question and in which church and state, intertwined since the days of Constantine, would begin to drift apart.

Martin Luther did not create the Reformation. The elements of such a movement were already in place, but Luther's zeal and force of personality served much like a match touched to a powder keg.

As a young man, Luther was overwhelmed by a sense of sin. He felt unable to confess his sins often or completely enough or to do enough penance to earn forgiveness. Then one day in about 1515, he happened to open the Bible to Romans 5:1: "Therefore, since we are justified by faith, we have peace with God through our Lord Jesus Christ."

Luther on Faith

The key point of Martin Luther's theology was that humans cannot achieve salvation by good deeds or through the intervention of earthly authority in the form of the church. Salvation, he said, can only come from faith.

In his "Introduction to St. Paul's Letter to the Romans," part of his translation of the Bible into German in 1522, Luther gave his definition of faith. This excerpt is found at www.iclnet.org:

"Faith is not what some people think it is. . . . 'Faith is not enough,' they say, 'You must do good works, you must be pious to be saved.'. . . Instead, faith is God's work in us, that changes us and gives new birth from God. It kills the Old Adam and makes us completely different people. It changes our hearts, our spirits, our thoughts and all our powers. It brings the Holy Spirit with it. Yes, it is a living, creative, active and powerful thing, this faith. Faith cannot help doing good works constantly. It doesn't stop to ask if good works ought to be done, but before anyone asks, it already has done them and continues to do them without ceasing. Anyone who does not do good works in this manner is an unbeliever. . . . Therefore, watch out for your own false ideas and guard against good-for-nothing gossips, who think they're smart enough to define faith and works, but really are the greatest of fools. Ask God to work faith in you, or you will remain forever without faith, no matter what you wish, say or can do."

Luther's views on salvation clashed with those of Catholicism.

Luther later wrote, "I felt that I had been born anew."[23] The concept that had occurred to him was that justification, or God's grace, cannot be earned by confession or penance or conferred by the church. It can come only as a gift from God to those he has chosen.

Luther's Word of God

Luther considered the Word of God, not the church, as the ultimate authority, but the Word of God, to Luther, was more than just the Bible. It was God himself. According to Luther, then, people should seek knowledge of God from the Word of God divinely inspired through the Bible. Moreover, they should seek God directly, without the church as an intermediary.

Luther was not saying the church was unnecessary. He thought it important that Christians exist within a body of faithful believers in communion with God. That church, however, is a creation of the Word of God, not the other way around. Therefore, the sacraments, or rites, administered by the church should be limited to those established by Jesus—baptism and Communion.

By denying that access to God was controlled by the church,

Luther rejected the basic validity of the concept of indulgences. He stated his case in dramatic fashion, nailing his document, the Ninety-five Theses, to the door of the cathe-

An engraving shows Martin Luther posting the Ninety-five Theses on the Wittenberg cathedral door, an event that launched the Protestant Reformation.

dral in Wittenberg on October 31, 1517. Unlike previous reformers, Luther had a means of widely disseminating his views—the printing press. Copies of the Ninety-five Theses were soon distributed throughout Germany, and one eventually reached the pope.

Reaction was swift. The pope first ordered Luther's monastic order, the Augustinians, to silence him. When Luther explained his views at the next Augustinian meeting, however, many of his fellow monks enthusiastically agreed with him.

Luther next was summoned to the empire's diet, as the conference of nobles was called, at Augsburg. He met there with the pope's representative but slipped away when he learned he might be arrested.

The "Wild Boar"

In the end, Luther's sponsorship by Frederick the Wise, ruler of the German state of Saxony, protected him. All the pope could manage was to issue, in 1520, a papal bull saying that "a wild boar has invaded thy [God's] vineyard"[24] and ordering all Luther's books to be burned. The outspoken monk responded by publicly burning a copy of the decree.

In 1521 Luther was summoned to another diet, this one in the city of Worms. The new emperor, Charles V, was a devout Catholic. He refused to debate the theological issues involved, only calling on Luther to disavow his viewpoint. "My conscience is a prisoner of God's word," Luther responded. "I cannot and will not recant, for to disobey one's conscience is neither just nor safe. God help me."[25]

Luther might well have been arrested except that Frederick the Wise anticipated his danger and had him smuggled to safety. The emperor was furious, but although he longed to extinguish Luther and his followers, he needed the support of Frederick and other German princes in his quarrels with France.

Such political factors allowed Lutheranism to spread and take firm root in many areas of Germany. When Charles attempted to outlaw the new movement, rulers of Lutheran states united in making a formal protest, thus gaining the name "Protestants." Eventually, Charles, needing the support of his nobles, agreed to the Peace of Nuremberg in 1532. In effect, the continued existence and growth of Protestantism was ensured.

Zwingli

This by no means ensured unity among adherents to Protestantism. A smaller but parallel Protestant movement took place in Switzerland, led by Ulrich Zwingli. Zwingli agreed with Luther that the Bible is the ultimate authority for Christians, but he went even further. Whereas Luther agreed to practices not specifically prohibited by scripture, such as music as part of worship, Zwingli rejected everything not specifically established in the Gospels.

The primary difference, and the one that eventually prevented the two groups from joining, was over the presence of Jesus in the sacrament of Communion. Luther denied transubstantiation—that the bread and wine of Communion become Jesus's flesh and blood. However, he thought some kind of divine interaction took place, that the body and blood are somehow in the bread and wine, a concept later called consubstantiation. Zwingli believed that the partaking of bread and wine, though an important part of worship, were symbolic only.

The likes of Luther and Zwingli put in place the foundations of the Protestant Reformation, but it fell to another to create the intellectual framework of the new faith. An introspective Frenchman who had little of the dazzling public presence of Luther, John Calvin, made a lasting impact on matters far beyond religion.

To Calvin, all people were inherently sinful because of the original fall from grace of Adam and Eve. He differed from Luther, however, in that he thought a spark of that grace still remains in everyone. Grace can be fully restored, he wrote, only by God—never by a person's own actions or by an outside agency such as the Catholic Church. Furthermore, God bestows his grace only on a small, predestined elect, with all the rest condemned to damnation.

The Struggle Against Sin

Even for the elect, however, grace can be withdrawn, so life, in Calvin's eyes, is a constant struggle against sin. Each person is to be conscious of his or her own sin, suffer its effects in humility, and strive in all things to reflect God's presence. "Our life is like a journey," he wrote. "[But] it is not God's will that we should march along casually as we please, but he sets the goal before us, and also directs us on the right way to it."[26]

Each of the elect, therefore, should live a life of sober piety. Furthermore, it is the responsibility of all believers to keep not only themselves but their neighbors and, as far as possible, the entire world on a straight and narrow spiritual

This engraving depicts John Calvin in his study. Calvin's version of the doctrine of predestination held that God has chosen only a few elect to achieve salvation.

path. It was not good enough to live according to God's law, but to do everything possible to bring about Jesus's earthly kingdom.

Calvin got a chance to put his preaching into practice in the Swiss city of Geneva, which in 1541 adopted his Ecclesiastical Ordinances, a document that set down in detail how men and women were to live in a city of God. What the ordinances required was a stern and, for the most part, joyless existence. Most games were prohibited, as were gambling and swearing. Taverns were strictly regulated. Colorful clothing was banned; church attendance was made compulsory. It was even against the law to give a child any but a biblical first name.

Calvin's Followers

Reformers throughout Europe flocked to Geneva to learn from Calvin and, despite the bleakness of his teachings, took them back with them. John Knox took them to Scotland in the form of Presbyterianism. In England, Calvin's disciples came to be known as Puritans, and the institution they carried to America became the Congregational Church. Many other Protestant denominations as varied as the Unitarians and the Baptists would adopt at least some of Calvin's doctrine.

The Reformation continued to spread, but the denominations that arose did not necessarily look anything like what Luther had envisioned. England's experience is an example. There, King Henry VIII, in order to obtain a marriage annulment that had been refused by the pope, broke from the Catholic Church and created a Church of England with himself as head. Henry

had no great love for Protestant theology and wanted the church to change in name only. Matters went far beyond what he intended, however, and the Church of England became and remained decidedly Protestant, as are its Anglican and Episcopal descendants.

The Catholic Church did not stand idly by and watch Protestantism grow. Its reaction, swift and often severe, is known as the Counter-Reformation. One aspect of this reaction was to identify and attack anyone whose beliefs did not conform to Catholic dogma, using a tribunal known as the Inquisition. Unlike the earlier Spanish Inquisition, whose chief targets were Jews and Muslims, the Roman Inquisition was established in 1542 specifically to fight Protestantism. The tribunal's members were empowered to seek out and ban writings and teachings considered heretical. Almost any discipline was apt to be examined for heresy. For example, the Inquisition's most famous trial was the condemnation in 1633 of astronomer Galileo Galilei for asserting that the earth moves around the sun.

The Jesuits

Another active part of Catholicism's reaction was to instill Catholic beliefs through education. For this task the church chose a cadre of priests known as the Society of Jesus, or Jesuits, founded by a former soldier named Ignatius of Loyola. The Jesuits set up schools and colleges for the training of both priests and laymen, but they also went secretly —and in great danger—into Protestant countries to minister to faithful Catholics.

The most far-reaching of the church's reaction to Protestantism was the Council of Trent, which met intermittently in that northern Italian city from 1545 to 1563. The actions of the council did much to reform the Catholic Church, condemning pluralism, requiring bishops to reside in their dioceses, regulating the use of indulgences, and

The Geneva Confession

John Calvin, when given complete authority over the Swiss city of Geneva, instituted a document known as the Geneva Confession, to which every citizen had to swear. The twenty-one articles covered everything from belief in God to obedience to church authority. These excerpts are found at www.creeds.net:

XII. Invocation of God Only and Intercession of Christ
As we have declared that we have confidence and hope for salvation and all good only in God through Jesus Christ, so we confess that we ought to invoke him in all necessities in the name of Jesus Christ, who is our Mediator and Advocate with him and has access to him. Likewise we ought to acknowledge that all good things come from him alone, and to give thanks to him for them. On the other hand, we reject the intercession of the saints as a superstition invented by men contrary to Scripture, for the reason that it proceeds from mistrust of the sufficiency of the intercession of Jesus Christ.

XIV. Sacraments
We believe that the sacraments which our Lord has ordained in his Church are to be regarded as exercises of faith for us, both for fortifying and confirming it in the promises of God and for witnessing before men. Of them there are in the Christian Church only two which are instituted by the authority of our Saviour: Baptism and the Supper of our Lord; for what is held within the realm of the pope concerning seven sacraments, we condemn as fable and lie.

The Council of Trent, shown in this sixteenth-century Italian painting, examined Roman Catholic doctrine and defined Catholicism for the next four hundred years.

establishing seminaries to improve education of priests.

The Council of Trent also examined almost every facet of Christianity in order to define what was and was not acceptable to the Catholic Church. Its findings, published in 1566, established Catholic doctrine for the next four hundred years.

The hardening of Catholicism toward Protestants was matched by a firm resolve by Protestants to resist all attempts to force them to surrender their beliefs. As a result, Europe was convulsed throughout the 1500s and 1600s by wars of religion. During these devastating conflicts—Christian against

Christian—an estimated 8 million people died.

Massacre in France

Violence in France was sporadic, depending on how much Protestant support the various French kings needed. When the anti-Protestant faction was in a position of strength, however, the results could be deadly. The most famous instance came on August 24, 1572, the eve of St. Bartholomew's Day. Convinced that the Huguenots, as French Protestants were known, were plotting to overthrow him, King Charles IX ordered that they should be attacked without warning. About two thousand Huguenots were killed in Paris and tens of thousands more throughout France in what came to be called the St. Bartholomew's Day Massacre.

The Council of Trent

The ultimate answer of the Roman Catholic Church to the challenges of the Protestant Reformation was the Council of Trent, which met on and off from 1543 to 1565. Its findings, which set the course of Catholicism for the next four hundred years, went into great detail as to what Catholics were to believe and how they were to worship. These canons, or laws, concerning justification, or salvation, are found at http://ic.net:

Canon IX. If any one saith, that by faith alone the impious is justified; in such wise as to mean, that nothing else is required to co-operate in order to the obtaining the grace of Justification, and that it is not in any way necessary, that he be prepared and disposed by the movement of his own will; let him be anathema [accursed].

Canon XVII. If any one saith, that the grace of Justification is only attained to by those who are predestined unto life; but that all others who are called, are called indeed, but receive not grace, as being, by the divine power, predestined unto evil; let him be anathema.

Canon XXIX. If any one saith, that he, who has fallen after baptism, is not able by the grace of God to rise again; or, that he is able indeed to recover the justice which he has lost, but by faith alone without the sacrament of Penance, contrary to what the holy Roman and universal Church—instructed by Christ and his Apostles—has hitherto professed, observed, and taught; let him be anathema.

In England, religious differences led to outright civil war. The Protestants, known as Puritans because of their desire to "purify" England's church from what they considered Catholic-like practices, went to war against King Charles I and those loyal to him. The war ranged back and forth over the country from 1642 to 1648, finally ending with the execution of Charles I on January 30, 1649.

By far the worst of the wars of religion, however, was the Thirty Years' War, fought in Germany from 1618 to 1648. It began as essentially a war between Protestant and Catholic princes in Germany but expanded into an international conflict. On one side was the house of Hapsburg, whose members ruled both Spain and the Holy Roman Empire. On the other were German Protestants and foreign countries, mostly Protestant but including Catholic France, which feared the growing power of the Hapsburgs. Before it was finally ended by the Peace of Westphalia, the war left much of Germany in ruins. Four-fifths of the population of Bohemia either had been killed or had fled the country.

Weary of religious warfare and appalled by the loss of life and economic devastation, the people of Europe began to question the va-lidity of ties between church and state and the necessity for all persons in the state to adhere to common religious beliefs. Slowly, in Protestant countries, at least, the idea of religious toleration began to take hold.

The Idea of Toleration

Toleration was a novel idea for Christians. Ever since the days of Constantine and Augustine of Hippo, a close partnership between church and state had been a fundamental principle, taken for granted as necessary to an orderly society. Moreover, the church should encompass a set of beliefs to be shared by all citizens. People thought that whatever kind of Christians they were—Catholic, Lutheran, or Puritan—there was only one correct form of Christianity, the one held by them.

Toleration, then, was slow to evolve and had to go through stages. The Peace of Westphalia adopted the principle that whatever was the ruler's religion should be that of the people. Under this live-and-let-live practice, a Catholic or Protestant German prince could demand his subjects follow his religion but would not try to impose it on a neighboring ruler of another faith.

One by one, the Protestant nations of Europe realized that their best interest was served if Christians, regardless of specific beliefs, could exist side by side. As one Englishman put it, "It is the union of interests and not of opinions that gives peace to kingdoms."[27]

Toleration did not necessarily mean that all religions within the state would be equal. Most countries still thought it necessary and proper to have an official religion. In some, membership in the state religion was required if one was to hold public office. In others, all persons had to contribute to the state religion whether they practiced it or not. Nowhere in Europe, however, was being without a religion an option.

Freedom in America
This final step in religious tolerance, freedom not only of religion but from religion, was taken in England's American colonies. The charter of the Commonwealth of Pennsylvania, written in 1701, said that no person was "at any time to be compelled to frequent or maintain any religious worship, place or ministry whatever, contrary to his or her mind."[28] For the first time since Constantine, fourteen hundred years earlier, Christianity and the secular state were separated.

The Protestant Reformation, Catholic Counter-Reformation, and wars of religion constituted a crisis from which Christianity emerged stronger than ever before. Christians, both Catholic and Protestant, looked at themselves and their world in new ways. These new viewpoints would make it possible for Christianity to undergo a dramatic expansion, in terms of both geography and the variety of ways in which Jesus's message was interpreted and put into practice.

chapter | seven

Expansion and Enlightenment

Prior to 1500 Christianity was shackled within both the geographic boundaries of Europe and the spiritual boundaries of religious orthodoxy. Then the chains were shattered. First, as European explorers discovered or rediscovered entire continents, Christianity spread faster in one century than it had in the previous fifteen. Then, following the Protestant Reformation, both Catholics and Protestants took their faiths in new and increasingly diverse directions.

Starting in about 1480 and over the next three hundred years, Christianity would be carried to virtually every corner of the world—by Spanish *conquistadores*, Portuguese traders, English pilgrims, and Protestant and Catholic missionaries. It would become the largest religion in the world, not only in terms of the number of believers but in the bewildering and constantly growing number of sects and denominations.

Before this Age of Exploration, Christianity was almost exclusively European, except for a few outposts such as the Coptic Church in Egypt and the tiny Church of St. Thomas in India. It was blocked by the Atlantic Ocean on the west, by Islam to the south and east, and by great stretches of barren steppes to the north of Russia.

The first hesitant steps at spreading the Christian faith were taken by the Portuguese, edging around the western coast of Africa in their tiny ships called caravels. Missionary work began in the Congo in 1482. The king there was baptized and renamed his capital city São Salvador, or "the savior."

Dividing the World

Most of Portugal's missionary work, however, would be among people far different from those in Africa. In 1493 Pope Alexander VI divided all heretofore unknown and unclaimed lands between Portugal and Spain. Spain had rights to the Americas, except for the eastern part of South America, what would later become Brazil. Portugal had Africa, India, and Asia.

Because of this territorial division, the Portuguese encountered, except in Africa, powerful, well-established societies whose religions—Buddhism, Taoism, Confucianism, Hinduism—were solidly entrenched. There was little opportunity for mass conversion. Instead, missionaries adapted themselves to the customs of the lands in which they found themselves, hoping that, by persuasion and by example, they could win converts.

The Portuguese were only moderately successful. Jesuit missionaries made the most headway in major coastal trading centers such as Goa and Madras in India, Canton and Shanghai in China, and Yokahama

Prior to 1500, one of the few Christian churches outside Europe was the Coptic Church in Egypt. Here, an ancient Coptic monastery stands in the desert near Cairo.

in Japan. However, they needed the support, or at least the permission, of local rulers in their efforts to win converts. Such permission was not always available. Most of the time, local rulers' reaction to Christian missionaries ranged from mild curiosity to indifference to outright hostility.

Because of the restrictions placed on the missionaries, Christianity never spread in Asia as it did in other parts of the world. Christian churches remained few, far between, and small. In the 1800s the Church of England would establish a presence in various reaches of the British Empire, but made little penetration into the native populations. In the mid-1990s, for example, fewer than 10 percent of the people of Asia were Christian.

The Americas

The situation was far different in the Americas, where the native population was easily overwhelmed by the Spanish in the south and, later, by the English and French in the north. When he divided the unknown world between Spain and Portugal, Alexander VI made it clear that he expected Christianity "may in all places be exalted, amplified, and enlarged . . . and the barbarous nations subdued and brought to the faith."[29]

The Spanish, however, were not as much concerned with spreading Christianity as with carving out an empire. They needed native labor, first to mine the gold and silver to be shipped back to Spain and later, when permanent colonies were established, to farm the land. The apostle Peter might have spoken of Christianity as a "brotherhood throughout the world" (1 Peter 5:9), but the Spanish overlords looked on the Indians as anything but equals. One priest, Tomás Ortiz, said, "They are stupid and silly. They are brutal. . . . Punishments have no effect on them."[30]

Had it not been for the appeals to Spain from some sympathetic priests, all the Indians might have become slaves. As it was, most were slaves in all but name. Instead of outright slavery, the Spanish established a system of forced labor called *encomienda*, or "assignment."

The Spanish informed the Indians of their status by reading to them a document called the *Requerimiento*, or "Requirement," which told them that the pope had granted their lands to Spain, that they were required to become Catholics and to work for the Spaniards, and that if they did not obey, the Spaniards would "take you and your wives and children, and shall make slaves of them, and . . . shall take

The conquered Aztecs are forced to build a palace for Spanish conquistador Hernán Cortes in this painting by Mexican artist Diego Rivera.

your goods and shall do you all the mischief and damage that we can."[31]

The Indians might protest, as did some chiefs in Colombia who said the pope "must have been drunk ... because what he gave was not his to give,"[32] but it made no difference.

Whether as slaves or forced laborers, the Indians of Mexico, Central America, and South America were Christianized, not by love, as Columbus would have preferred, but by whip and gun. As a result, Latin America became and would remain

The Spanish Conquests

Frequently the conquerors of the New World cared more about wealth than converting natives. Spanish priest Bartolomé de Las Casas wrote a severe indictment of his countrymen. This excerpt is found at www.americanjourney.psmedia.com:

"That which led the Spaniards to these unsanctified impieties was the desire of Gold, to make themselves suddenly rich, for the obtaining of dignities & honours which were no way fit for them. In a word, their covetousness, their ambition, which could not be more in any people under heaven, the riches of the Countrey, and the patience of the people gave occasion to this their devillish barbarism. For the Spaniards so contemned them [held them in contempt] (I now speak what I have seen without the least untruth) that they used them not like beasts, for that would have been tolerable, but looked upon them as if they had been but the dung and filth of the earth, and so little they regarded the health of their souls, that they suffered this great multitude to die without the least light of Religion; neither is this lesse true than what I have said before and that which those tyrants themselves dare not deny, without speaking a notorious fallhood [falsehood], that the Indians never gave them the least cause to offer them violence, but received them as Angels sent from heaven, till their excessive cruelties, the torments and slaughters of their Countrymen mov'd them to take Armes against the Spaniards."

overwhelmingly Roman Catholic. About 92 percent of the region's population practiced that religion in the 1990s.

France and England

The Indians were not the only people who took issue with the pope's division of the world. France and England likewise were not ready to cede the Americas and their riches to Catholic neighbors. When they eventually challenged Spain in the Americas—the French starting in Nova Scotia in 1605 and the English in Virginia in 1607—Spain could not prevent them. Consequently, the religious settlement of North America was far different than in the south.

French Catholic missionaries began arriving in Canada in 1615, and their work among the Indians consisted more of education and health care than forced conversion. They were aided by the fact that French settlers were more interested in the fur trade than in mining or agriculture; thus there was little need for the Indians as a workforce.

The relatively benevolent attitude of the French missionaries served to make the eastern portion of Canada solidly Roman Catholic, and it has largely remained so. When Great Britain took over Canada in 1763, it had no wish to try to abolish Catholicism, but western Canada, settled mostly by the English would contain a large Protestant majority.

The roles played by religion in the settlement of the thirteen English colonies that eventually would become the United States varied from paramount to almost negligible. Some colonists were fleeing religious persecution and wanted a place in which they could freely follow their beliefs. Others came out of a desire to make more prosperous lives for themselves and their families.

Most of those in the first group settled in New England, beginning in 1620 with the landing of a group of Puritans

in Plymouth, Massachusetts. They were later joined by thousands of others, refugees from persecution by the Church of England.

To the Puritans, however, religious freedom did not include toleration of other faiths. In 1636 a Massachusetts minister, Roger

A woodcut shows French priests preaching to Indians in North America. The French seldom attempted conversion by force.

Roger Williams

Starting in the early 1600s, thousands of Puritans fled religious persecution in England and settled in North America. There, they were free to practice their religion, but they did not extend that same freedom to others.

When a young Congregationalist minister named Roger Williams preached toleration, he was banished from the Massachusetts Colony and founded Rhode Island. He wrote about persecution in a 1644 tract titled The Bloudy Tenet. *This excerpt is found at www.worldpolicy.org:*

"Breech of civil peace may arise when false and idolatrous practices are held forth, and yet no breach of civil peace from the doctrine or practice, or the manner of holding forth, but from that wrong and preposterous way of suppressing, preventing, and extinguishing such doctrines or practices by weapons of wrath and blood, whips, stocks, imprisonment, banishment, death, & by which men commonly are persuaded to convert heretics, and to cast out unclean spirits, which only the finger of God can do, that is, the mighty power of the Spirit in the word. Hence the town is in an uproar, and the country takes the alarm to expel that fog or mist of error, heresy, blasphemy, as is supposed, with swords and guns. Whereas it is light alone, even light from the bright shining Sun of Righteousness, which is able, in the souls and consciences of men to dispel and scatter such fogs and darkness."

Williams, was banished for advocating complete freedom of worship. He and some followers founded the colony of Providence, which in 1644 became Rhode Island.

Religious Freedom

Rhode Island thus became the first of the colonies to allow religious freedom. It would be followed in 1681, when William Penn established Pennsylvania, which was originally intended as a refuge for the sect known as Quakers but which permitted free worship.

The southern colonies—Virginia, the Carolinas, and Georgia—were founded largely out of a desire for profit rather than for reasons of conscience. Consequently, the prevailing and official religion tended to be the Church of England, although there were many Quakers and Baptists within the poorer classes.

Maryland was the lone North American colony established for Catholics. In 1632 England's King Charles I, seeking Catholic support, granted rights over part of northern Virginia to a prominent Catholic, Lord Baltimore.

However, religious intolerance —even in Puritan New England— never was as intense as in Europe. The need for new settlers of whatever faith and a frontier spirit created a society that would be able, in its constitution, to establish complete freedom of religion.

Just as western European culture achieved worldwide dominance as a result of colonization from 1500 to 1900, so did Christianity come to be the world's most prominent religion, taking in 33 percent of the total population. Its members are in the majority on every continent except Asia, and in Europe, Latin America, North America, and Oceania, its members exceed 75 percent of the population.

At almost the same time that Christianity was experiencing dramatic geographical expansion, it was undergoing a proliferation of ways in which Christians proclaimed their faith. Whereas the Christianity of Constantine's era or even that of Luther might have had two or three principal doctrines vying for supremacy, the freedom of thought emerging from the Protestant Reformation had caused Christianity to divide, redivide, and subdivide into a complex matrix of sects and denominations.

Rationalism

Part of what drove this diversification was a change in the way people viewed religion—and knowledge —in general. The wars of religion had been fought in part over issues that could not be proved one way or another—matters of faith. Afterward, a movement grew up to approach theology in a more rational way, to substitute reason for faith in an attempt to answer theological questions. This spirit of inquiry, stemming from the rediscovery of the works of Aristotle and expressed in the writings of Thomas Aquinas, was known as rationalism.

One of the earliest proponents of rationalism was the French philosopher René Descartes, who "proved" the existence of God by reasoning that, since a human mind is incapable of imagining a more perfect being, the idea must have been put there by God. England's John Locke agreed with Descartes to a point but held that knowledge is derived from experience in addition to insight.

The eventual outgrowth of rationalism was deism. The Deists

French philosopher René Descartes claimed that rational thought could prove the existence of God.

stripped Christianity to its core: belief in God, worship of God, leading an ethical life. They believed that God created the universe and allows it to run according to natural, reasonable law, much like a person does after having wound a clock.

Rationalism continued to win adherents, mostly among the highly educated. Elements have survived to the present, for example, in the Unitarian Universalist Church, which believes that "personal experience, conscience and reason should be the final authorities in religion, and that in the end religious authority lies not in a book or person or institution, but in ourselves."[33] For the most part, however, the rationalist movement was coldly intellectual, diminishing the importance and the immediacy of Jesus and holding little appeal for the vast majority of Christians.

Spiritualism and Pietism

The reactions to rationalism, as well as to strict, confining dogma, both Catholic and Protestant, were Spiritualism and Pietism. It has been from these two movements, principally Pietism, that many of today's most prominent Protestant denominations have sprung. They had many strong, influential voices, but three will suffice to illustrate the impact they had on Christianity:

George Fox, John Wesley, and George Whitefield.

The Spiritualist movement was exemplified by Fox, an English cobbler's apprentice who rejected the outward manifestations of Christianity —churches, ministers, and sacraments such as baptism—as necessary for a person to find God. Instead, he said, each person has an "inner light" that, if followed, will lead to a knowledge of God and to salvation. He thus rejected the idea held by Lutherans and Calvinists that only a small number of Christians are

John Wesley

An Anglican priest who doubted his own faith, John Wesley underwent a personal conversion experience in 1748. He became convinced that the only way to salvation was by faith and that Jesus works through the heart of those who seek him.

Wesley meant for his movement—Methodism—to remain within the Church of England, but it became separate and today is one of the largest Protestant denominations. This excerpt from one of Wesley's sermons is found at www.godrules.net:

"What faith is it then through which we are saved? It may be answered, first, in general, it is a faith in Christ: Christ, and God through Christ, are the proper objects of it. Herein, therefore, it is sufficiently, absolutely distinguished from the faith either of ancient or modern heathens. And from the faith of a devil it is fully distinguished by this: it is not barely a speculative, rational thing, a cold, lifeless assent, a train of ideas in the head; but also a disposition of the heart. For thus saith the Scripture, 'With the heart man believeth unto righteousness;' and, 'If thou shalt confess with thy mouth the Lord Jesus, and shalt believe in thy heart that God hath raised him from the dead, thou shalt be saved.'"

marked for salvation, the dependence on clergy and ritual of the Catholics and Anglicans, and the entire reliance on reason.

Fox began to preach in 1649, often interrupting worship services of established churches to announce his vision. At times bodily ejected, beaten, stoned, and imprisoned, he nevertheless attracted a following. Fox named his group the Society of Friends, but they came to be known as Quakers because they were said to tremble from religious zeal. Their often disruptive behavior and their strict pacifism led to persecution in Great Britain, and thousands of followers migrated to America.

John Wesley

The Quakers' extremism kept them from becoming a major force in Christianity. Less extreme—and immensely more powerful and influential—have been the Methodists, an offshoot of the Pietist movement. This influence has established Methodism's founder, John Wesley, as perhaps—after Luther and Calvin —the most important person in Protestant history.

Wesley became an Anglican priest in 1728 but, while a missionary in America, began to doubt the sincerity of his faith. He was disturbed that he had experienced no personal, inward message of salvation from Jesus.

Back in England, he experienced his own personal conversion in 1738. Thus inwardly assured of his own salvation, he set out to work for the salvation of others. He had no desire to start a new church; he wanted to work within the Church of England to bring a new concept of faith to its members.

While at Oxford, he had joined a small religious society with his younger brother Charles and some other students. They vowed among themselves to lead righteous lives and devote so many hours a week to charity, so many to study, and so many to prayer. The group's resolve to seek God by "rule and method" caused fellow students to mock them as "methodists." When Wesley began attracting followers through his preaching, the name was revived and stuck.

Methodism, now with a worldwide membership estimated at 70 million, succeeded because it had wide appeal to the people of both Great Britain and the United States in the second half of the 1700s. The British were experiencing the Industrial Revolution, and the masses of people moving to urban areas felt disconnected with the old way of life, including the Anglican church.

Methodism provided them a belief system and spoke to their need for individuality. Americans, as they moved westward in increasing numbers, lost contact with the established churches but heeded the emotional appeal of the circuit-riding Methodist preachers.

Parallel Movements

Wesley and Methodism were part of a parallel religious phenomenon on both sides of the Atlantic. It has been known as the Evangelical Movement in Europe and the Great Awakening in the United States and was the culmination of the reaction against rationalism. The rationalists sought to arrive at an intellectual understanding and acceptance of the Christian message. Those touched by this new movement felt as if they had been personally seized by God and brought face-to-face with salvation. European and American Christianity was gripped by an excitement unknown since Luther.

George Whitefield

In an era known for emotional preaching, George Whitefield stood out as one of the most powerful speakers. The last sermon Whitefield preached in London before his final trip to America was titled "The Good Shepherd." This excerpt is found at www.oakharbor.net:

"And as Christ has given us eternal life, O my brethren, some of you, I doubt not, will be gone to him before my return; but, my dear brethren, my dear hearers, never mind that; we shall part, but it will be to meet again for ever. . . . God grant that none that weep now at my parting, may weep at our meeting at the day of judgment; and if you never were among Christ's sheep before, may Christ Jesus bring you now. O come, come, see what it is to have eternal life; do not refuse it; haste, sinner, haste away: may the great, the good Shepherd, draw your Souls. Oh! If you never heard his voice before, God grant you may hear it now; that I may have this comfort when I am gone, that I had the last time of my leaving you, that some souls are awakened at the parting sermon. O that it may be a farewell sermon to you; that it may be a means of your taking a farewell of the world, the lust of the flesh, the lust of the eye, and the pride of life. O come! Come! Come! To the Lord Jesus Christ; to him I leave you."

In America, that excitement came as the result of fiery sermons in which preachers exhorted eager listeners to repent and be reborn in Jesus's spirit. Perhaps the most eloquent of these preachers was George Whitefield.

Whitefield had been a member of Wesley's group at Oxford and had gone on to become famous throughout England for his preaching, often outdoors, to audiences numbering in the thousands. He and Wesley joined forces for a time, but when they could not agree on the doctrine of predestination—Whitefield accepted it and Wesley rejected it—they parted ways.

Once in America, Whitefield traveled throughout the colonies, preaching to huge and enthusiastic crowds. He whipped his listeners into a frenzy and had them shouting, weeping, and fainting as the spirit moved them. Conservative ministers were dubious. William Smith, an Anglican priest in Philadelphia, called the reaction "an instantaneous sort of conversion" in which the converted "mistake their own Enthusiasm for the inward Operation of the holy Spirit."[34]

Though others might dismiss them as demagogues, the preachers of the Evangelical Movement and the Great Awakening breathed new life and energy into Christianity. The fervor of many of today's Protestant churches, both traditional denominations and fundamentalist groups such as the Pentecostals, can be traced to the movement. It invigorated the old and invited the new. This intensely personal character of Christianity has carried through to today. Yet even though the central message—the soul's salvation through Jesus—remains at the core of the faith, the modern era has witnessed a tremendous and sometimes bewildering variety in what Christians believe and how they turn belief into practice.

chapter | eight

Beliefs and Worship

England's Queen Elizabeth I, frustrated by the continuing strife between Catholics and Protestants in her country, once exclaimed, "There is only one Christ, Jesus, one faith. All else is a dispute over trifles."[35] There are, indeed, beliefs that are central to Christianity, though few would dismiss the sacraments, doctrine, and practices of the church—over which wars have been fought and people tortured and killed—as trifles. Moreover, it is these "trifles" that give the many fruits on the Christian tree their flavor and color the way in which the beliefs are proclaimed in worship.

At their heart, many Christian beliefs are contained in one of the oldest statements of Christian faith, the Apostles' Creed, parts of which date from about A.D. 150. At the same time this statement of faith can be—and has been—the source of vigorous disagreement.

The creed begins with the deceptively simple statement "I believe in God, the Father Almighty, creator of heaven and earth."[36] The nature of this God, however, is scarcely a simple thing to define. Most Christians would agree that their God is the God depicted in the first book of the Bible, Genesis. Moreover—and a much more difficult concept for Christians to grasp—God is seen as the ultimate reality of which all things are part. As such, God is eternal; he has existed prior to creation and will exist after the end of time, whenever and however that may come to be.

The Immediate God

To most Christians, God is not only a creator, but also a God who takes a day-to-day interest in what has been created. Even though they concede that he may no longer hold face-to-face talks as the Bible says he did with Abraham and Moses, they believe he is always present, can be communicated with through prayer, and can use humanity to work his will. As Oxford University theologian Maurice Wiles put it, "God is no absentee landlord; he is present reality."[37]

This last concept of an active, present God is how some theologians interpret the idea of the Holy Spirit, through which the Apostles' Creed says Jesus was conceived. Some Christians, notably Roman Catholics, believe that God's gifts to humanity—such as wisdom, courage, knowledge, piety—are aspects of the Holy Spirit.

The Apostles' Creed goes on to say that Christians "believe in Jesus Christ, God's only son, our Lord, who was conceived by the Holy Spirit, born of the Virgin Mary, suffered under Pontius Pilate, was crucified, died, and was buried." This very straightforward statement is meant to underscore Jesus's humanity—that he was a real person, had a real mother, lived at a real time, and died a real, human death. The passage was included in response to a few early Christians who held that Jesus was wholly divine.

The Virgin Birth

The virgin birth is an idea that, in an age in which miracles are not considered commonplace, is difficult for many Christians to accept. Some critics claim the reference was included in the Apostles' Creed both to enhance the idea of Jesus's divinity and to solidify his status as the fulfillment of Isaiah's prophecy. Like many other aspects of Christianity, including the Resurrection, the virgin birth remains a matter of faith rather than historically verifiable fact.

Christians do not believe that Jesus was God's son in the same sense as the ancient Greeks and Romans believed that offspring could result from physical unions of gods and mortals. Jesus is not, then, a demigod. Rather, he is related to Mary only in that he obtains from her his humanity, which nevertheless is real, not just an abstraction.

The issue is further complicated by the concept, central to most of

Christianity, that Jesus is also God, part of the Trinity of Father, Son, and Holy Spirit. Jesus, then, coexisted with God before he was born, and God coexisted with Jesus during the latter's time on earth. The entire question of the nature of God, Jesus, the Holy Spirit, and the Trinity have engendered thousands of opinions and millions of words over the history of Christianity. Some theologians say simply that the concept is beyond human understanding, and most Christians are willing to let it go at that.

The Resurrection

The Apostles' Creed says that Jesus "descended to the dead. On the third day [after his death] he rose again; he ascended into heaven." The Resurrection is at the very heart of Christian belief. Christians believe that Jesus rose from the dead, not totally as a spirit, but at least partially flesh and blood. On one hand, the Bible says he suddenly appeared among the disciples as if he were a spirit, but on the other hand, he ate with them and had them touch him to demonstrate his reality.

The classic Christian belief, therefore—as stated later in the Apostles' Creed—is the "resurrection of the body." This means that all those who after death achieve salvation through God's grace will, like

The Apostles' Creed

The Apostles' Creed, recited each Sunday in Christian churches around the world, got its name from the legend that, on the day of Pentecost, each of Jesus's twelve disciples contributed one article that, when taken together, would constitute a summary of the faith. Most scholars, however, think the creed developed over several centuries. Indeed, the final form used today dates from the 500s.

In the early church, when Christians were being persecuted by the Roman government, people seeking to be baptized were asked to memorize the creed. The early Christians did not want the details of their religion written down and spread to those that might mock them.

For many centuries, those to be baptized would recite the creed, usually just before Easter. Since the Apostles' Creed is much shorter than the other main statement of Christianity, the Nicene Creed, it has remained the most popular for those studying to become Christians.

A fresco by Fra Angelico portrays an angel telling women that the crucified Jesus has risen from his tomb. Jesus's resurrection is central to Christianity.

Jesus, somehow again have a bodily existence. Furthermore, again in the words of the creed, resurrected Christians will enjoy "life everlasting."

The Bible refers to both "heaven" and "paradise" but says little about of what each consists. It is even unclear whether they are the same place or, indeed, if they exist as "places" at all. Certainly the writers of the Bible imagined heaven as a literal place, as

can be seen from the many references to things "ascending to" or "coming down from" heaven. In the book of John, Jesus portrays heaven as a house with many rooms that will be prepared for the faithful.

Conversely, the other possibility of afterlife, according to the Bible, is hell, normally pictured, as in Revelations 20:10, as a "lake of fire and sulphur where [the unsaved] will be tormented day and night for ever and ever." Painters throughout history have eagerly embellished this image, constructing landscapes of fire and brimstone where the damned are tortured by pitchfork-wielding devils.

The Judgment

The Apostles' Creed says that it will be Jesus who will decide who enters heaven, in whatever form it may be, when he returns to "judge the living and the dead." According to Roman Catholic doctrine, this will be a final judgment, but possibly not the only judgment. In Catholic theology, a person after death receives what is called a "particular judgment," whereby their souls may enter heaven, hell, or the temporary state called purgatory, a place for those whose sins are not serious enough to consign them to hell but too serious to allow them immediate entrance into heaven.

The "final judgment" or "last judgment" will occur on Jesus's return,

The Descent into Hell

Many translations of both the Apostles' Creed and the Nicene Creed contain the statement that, after his death on the cross, Jesus "descended into hell." This has puzzled many modern Christians, used to thinking of hell as a place where those who have lived evil lives are tortured for eternity.

The passage, however, does not refer to the hell of the damned, but to Hades (in Greek) or Sheol (in Hebrew), the realm of the dead. In this place, according to Roman Catholicism, the dead exist without a vision of God, awaiting their deliverance by Jesus.

Also raising questions is the statement "On the third day he rose again." The Gospel of Matthew (12:40) quotes Jesus as saying, "For as Jonah was three days and three nights in the belly of a huge fish, so the Son of Man will be three days and three nights in the heart of the earth."

Some people say the passage in Matthew should be taken literally, and thus they do not observe the Crucifixion on what Christianity calls Good Friday, believing instead that Jesus's death took place on a Wednesday. Others, however, point to another passage in Matthew (17:23) in which Jesus says, "The Son of Man is going to be betrayed into the hands of men. They will kill him, and *on* the third day he will be raised to life."

sometimes referred to as the Second Coming. At this time, Catholics believe, all the souls in purgatory will be released into heaven and all persons still living will be judged. Also at this time, the bodies of the dead will be resurrected and reunited with their souls.

Protestants, on the other hand, reject the idea of purgatory. Many believe that, on death, the body decays and the soul goes into a state of unawareness. At the last judgment, those souls are called forth, given some sort of bodily existence, and sent to heaven or hell. Others, however, think that the assignment to the afterlife takes place immediately after death.

The Liberal View

A more liberal Protestant view of the Christian afterlife is that a person's soul, not the body, is eternal. In this view, the soul existed prior to being born into a human body and, if the person achieves salvation, will return to God. As Paul wrote (1 Corinthians 15:50–53):

Flesh and blood cannot inherit the kingdom of God, nor does the perishable inherit the imperishable. Lo! I tell you a mystery. We shall not all sleep, but we shall all be changed, in a mo-

ment, in the twinkling of an eye, at the last trumpet. For the trumpet will sound, and the dead will be raised imperishable, and we shall be changed. For this perishable nature must put on the imperishable, and this mortal nature must put on immortality.

For many Christians today, Paul's "imperishable" is the soul. Heaven, therefore, would be the rejoining of the soul with God and Jesus and its presence with them forever. Hell, on the other hand, would be the existence of the soul in a void, deprived of the presence of God.

The Apostles' Creed also proclaims belief in the "communion of saints," a reference to the religious practices, most of them embodied in worship services, known as the sacraments. How many sacraments there are has been a matter for debate over the centuries, but Roman Catholics recognize seven—baptism; Communion; confirmation, or admission to the church; penance, or the act of confessing sins and receiving forgiveness; ordination, or the ceremony through which priests or bishops are certified; extreme unction, a ceremony of healing or performing the last rites to prepare a person for death; and marriage.

A person's soul hovers over its deceased body in this illustration by William Blake. Many Christians believe in a bodily, rather than purely spiritual, resurrection.

Catholics regard all of these sacraments as effective and some of them as essential. Baptism is necessary to salvation, for instance. Communion and confession are required, and no marriage except that within the church is recognized. Some Protestant churches, such as the Anglican and Lutheran, have retained most of the Catholic sacraments to some degree. In the Anglican Church, for instance, confession may be made individually to a priest but more often is done through a communal recitation. The majority of Protestant churches, however, recognize only two sacraments—baptism and Communion.

In most Christian churches, the sacraments have been woven into the fabric of worship carried out, for the most part, on Sundays throughout the world. The earliest Christians gathered on Saturday, the Jewish Sabbath, but by the second century a prominent bishop, Justin Martyr, explained that Sunday was the holy day "because it is the first day on which God, having wrought a change in the darkness and matter, made the world; and Jesus Christ, our Saviour, on the same day rose from the dead."[38]

The Jewish Foundation

Christian worship, nevertheless, is based on the Jewish liturgy, or the prescribed order of service. All Christian churches that follow such established worship patterns are known as liturgical churches and include Roman Catholicism and Protestant churches, such as the Anglican and Lutheran, that have retained major parts of the Catholic liturgy.

Worship in liturgical churches generally follows two liturgies—the Liturgy of the Word and the Liturgy of the Eucharist. The Liturgy of the Word is a direct descendant of Jewish practice, in which the service consisted of singing, prayers, readings from sacred texts, and comment on the readings from either the rabbi (or "teacher") or a member of the congregation.

The Christian Liturgy of the Word consists of these same general elements. While there are numerous variations, the liturgy of the Episcopal Church, the primary Anglican Church in the United States, provides a representative example. After an opening hymn and procession into the church, the priest issues a call to worship. Various texts may be recited or sung, including the Gloria Patri ("Glory Be to the Father") or the Kyrie Eleison ("Christ

Baptism

Except perhaps for Communion, the most solemn ceremony of the Christian church is baptism. Many regard it as much more than a simple welcoming of a person into the church. They see it instead as a burial of the old self and a rebirth in Jesus.

Exactly how baptism is to be performed has been and remains a point of contention. Some maintain that the only valid baptism is by complete immersion in water. In many denominations, however, the priest or minister sprinkles or pours a small amount of water on the head of the person being baptized.

According to the Bible, Jesus was baptized by his cousin John in the Jordan River. The gospels are not clear about whether or not this involved total immersion. Mark (1:10) says, for example, "when he came up out of the water." Some representations through the centuries have shown Jesus standing waistdeep in the river while John pours water on him.

Those who argue for immersion, however, point to the Greek word for baptize, *baptizein*, which is translated as "to dip." This proves, they say, that Jesus was dipped completely under the surface of the water and therefore set a pattern that all Christians must follow.

Have Mercy"), both of which are also part of the Catholic tradition.

Next come two or more readings, at least one each from the Epistles and Gospels. Hymns are normally sung between readings, or a psalm may be read or sung.

The Sermon

Next comes the sermon, which varies considerably in length depending on the tradition of various denominations. In the Catholic Church, the sermon is called a homily, and it may last only five minutes. The sermon is usually somewhat longer—fifteen to twenty minutes—in Episcopal and Lutheran churches, and in some other Protestant churches, it may take up half or more of the entire service—thirty to forty-five minutes or longer.

The sermon, the equivalent of the Jewish commentary on readings, played a minor role or was absent altogether in the medieval Catholic Church; at the time it was not considered necessary for the clergy to try to explain God's word to the people. That changed with the Protestant Reformation and particularly with the translation of the Bible into languages ordinary people could read. During the Evangelical Movement and the Great Awakening, people came by the thousands to listen to clergymen like George Whitefield preach for hours on end. Today many Protestant churches, especially in more fundamentalist denominations, are known for their lengthy, highly emotional sermons.

In the Episcopal church, after the sermon, the congregation recites the Nicene Creed, followed by a series of prayers, followed in turn by the communal confession of sin and the granting of forgiveness, in Jesus's name, by the priest.

The "Peace"

Ancient Christian ceremonies included a kiss of peace, in which the people greeted one another in Jesus's name. In most Episcopal churches, this brief interlude following the confession is now a handshake with persons close by accompanied by a phrase such as, "Peace be with you." The Liturgy of the Word normally ends with the passing of collection plates for monetary offerings, a feature of virtually every Christian service and one that dates from the earliest days when the first Christians gave all their possessions to the common good.

The Liturgy of the Eucharist that follows is considered the most important part of worship in liturgical churches but does not hold as important a place in denominations that conduct less structured services. Yet, by whatever name it is called —Eucharist, Communion, Lord's Supper—it is a part of almost every denomination's or sect's worship.

For all its near-universal practice, Communion is also the sacrament that has caused some of the most bitter divisions in Christianity over the centuries. The Eucharist commemorates the last meal eaten by Jesus and his disciples prior to his arrest and the sacrificing of himself and taking upon himself the sins of all humanity. Paul, as well as the authors of the Gospels, quote Jesus as having specifically said "my body" and "my blood" when referring to the bread and wine. For this reason, the Roman Catholic Church teaches that the bread, or wafers, and wine are literally transformed—transubstantiated—into Jesus's body and blood at the time they are consecrated by the priest, even though they do not change in outward appearance.

Different Views

Most Protestants, however, hold different and widely varying views. Some churches, such as the Anglican and Lutheran, believe in consubstantiation, whereby the body and blood of Jesus enter the bread and wine and coexist. Still other Protestants believe that Jesus is present at the Eucharist, but only in a spiritual sense, while others regard the bread and wine only as symbols of Jesus's sacrifice. To many modern Christians, the differences may seem unimportant, but history is full of accounts of people burned at the stake for their beliefs about the Eucharist.

The Eucharist is by no means the same from church to church, in either frequency or substance. The majority of Protestant denominations may conduct the Eucharist monthly or even less frequently. Others, however, insist that weekly communion was called for when Jesus said (1 Corinthians 11:25), "Do this, as often as you drink it, in remembrance of me." The other major issue involves the use of wine; Protestant denominations that teach abstinence from alcoholic drinks use grape juice instead.

All worship practices—hymns, prayers, readings, sermons, confession, Eucharist—can be found in some combination in virtually all Christian churches, but there are many exceptions, and the exceptions go from one extreme to the other. On one hand, for example, Quaker meetings have no ministers, no music, no recited prayers, no sermon, no Eucharist. Instead, mem-

Christianity in the United States

In the American Religious Identity Survey conducted in 2001, 76.5 percent of respondents identified themselves as Christians. The next highest number, 13.2 percent, said they were nonreligious. Judaism was the only other religion claiming more than 1 percent.

The largest number of Christians in the United States, 24.5 percent, were Roman Catholics. Baptists were next at 16.3 percent, followed by Methodists (6.8), Lutherans (4.6), Presbyterians (2.7), Pentecostals (2.1), and Episcopalians (1.7).

Another report in 2001, this by the *Yearbook of American and Canadian Churches*, showed a total Roman Catholic membership in the United States of 62.3 million. Southern Baptists were by far the largest Protestant denomination at 19.8 million, followed by Methodists (8.3 million), Latter-day Saints, or Mormons (5.3), Evangelical Lutherans (5.0), Church of God in Christ (5.0), Presbyterian (3.5), National Baptist (3.5), Assemblies of God (2.6), and Missouri Synod Lutherans (2.5).

Southern Baptists had more churches in the United States (37,893) than any other group, followed by the Methodists (37,203) and Roman Catholics (22,400).

bers sit in silent, contemplative prayer. Sometimes people are moved to speak; sometimes not. At the other extreme are the nonliturgical churches categorized under the umbrella name of Pentecostalism. Services tend to be highly emotional, and may include glossolalia, or speaking in unknown languages, and healing ceremonies.

In his discussion of Christian beliefs, Oxford professor of divinity Maurice Wiles recalled the Latin adage *Quot hominess, tot sententiae* (There are as many opinions as there are people). Indeed, there is a degree of individuality in both belief and worship that would have been considered impossible prior to the Protestant Reformation.

Belief and worship, however, are not confined to Sundays. At the end of the Episcopal service, the priest says, "And now, Father, send us out to do the work you have given us to do, to love and serve you as faithful witnesses of Christ our Lord."[39] The challenge for Christians has always been to take Jesus's message and put it to work in everyday life, and the challenges have seldom been greater than in the present.

chapter nine

Christianity in the New Millennium

Christianity was the most powerful force in the world of medieval Europe. Carried by those European nations, it became the dominant religion of the world by the 1800s. Those worlds have passed on, and Christianity in the twenty-first century faces stern challenges, both from within and without. Even as it seeks to bring Jesus's teaching to bear on social and economic problems, it is beset with serious problems of its own.

Christianity's challenges are many, but the primary ones can be sorted into three areas. First, the sexual revolution of the latter third of the twentieth century is having a dramatic effect. Second, churches, which for many years stood aloof from politics, have taken an increasingly active and sometimes dangerous role. Third, the world has become more secular, less awed by the mysteries of religion, more skeptical, and less inclined to accept authority.

One of Christianity's sharpest debates is over the question of women clergy. Ever since 1853, when Antoinette Brown was ordained by the Congregationalist Church in Wayne County, New York, women have been making slow but steady inroads into what was previously an exclusively male domain. Many of the largest Protestant denominations—Presbyterian, United Methodist, Lutheran, United Church of Christ—have had women ministers for decades. They have been joined more recently by the Anglican churches. In one denomination, the Unitarian Universalists, women clergy are in the majority.

The Catholic Prohibition

The Roman Catholic Church forbids women from becoming priests and does not recognize the few who have been ordained in isolated instances by reform-minded bishops. There are no female clergy, either, in the Orthodox churches. In addition, most very conservative, fundamentalist Protestant denominations do not ordain women, including the Southern Baptist Convention, the largest Protestant denomination in the United States. The official Southern Baptist stance is that, even though the Bible teaches that women are equal in value to men, the role of ordained minister is assigned only to men.

The issue of women clergy continues to be divisive, even within some of the Christian denominations in which they serve. Opponents point to biblical references such as

Janith M. Otte-Murphy (left) is congratulated after her ordination in 1977 as the first female minister in the Association of Evangelical Lutheran Churches.

One Woman's Struggle

Women who feel themselves called to become Catholic priests often face an internal struggle between their desire to fulfill their hopes and the Catholic prohibition of women clergy. One such woman, Colette Joyce, a pastoral minister in London but not ordained into the priesthood, wrote about her dilemma in 1999. This excerpt is found at www.womenpriests.org:

"The publication of 'Ordinatio Sacerdotalis' in 1994, restating that the Church has no authority to confer priestly ordination on women and that there is, therefore, no further need for discussion on the matter, has increased the acuteness of my dilemma. For me, it happened that the occasion of experiencing a call to priesthood was also my deepest experience of God. . . .

"It is painful to be told repeatedly in Church documents that the vocation to which I believe God is calling me is illegitimate, when it is that very vocation that has driven me to service within the Church in the first place! When I preach, or preside at a communion service, or take on a new responsibility, or speak out on some issue, I am always wondering whether what I have said or how I have acted is okay for me as a woman who is NOT a priest (but who would like to be). All the time it feels like the emphasis is on being careful about what I can't do, rather that on what service I can give which would be to the greater glory of God. It shouldn't have to be like that."

1 Timothy 2:11–12: "Let a woman learn in silence with all submissiveness. I permit no woman to teach or to have authority over men; she is to keep silent."

Opponents also cite 1 Corinthians 14:34–35: "The women should keep silence in the churches. For they are not permitted to speak, but should be subordinate, as even the law says. If there is anything they desire to know, let them ask their husbands at home. For it is shameful for a woman to speak in church." They also say that Jesus set the example for all time by choosing only men as his disciples.

Paul's Opinion?

Those who advocate women clergy counter that these quotations reflect only Paul's opinion. Furthermore, they say, Paul himself wrote in Galatians 3:28, "There is no longer male and female; for all of you are one in Christ Jesus," suggesting that even Paul might have countenanced women clergy.

Some women, such as United Church of Christ minister Ruth Brandon Minter, reject scriptural denial of women clergy, charging instead that "many men feel extremely threatened by a woman holding that degree of power and influence over church life."[40]

And Wesleyan Church minister Patricia David warns, "We should always be careful about putting God in a box and determining exactly how He should and should not go about His business of spreading the Gospel. God bestows His gifts as He chooses, and it is not always in accordance with what we expect."[41]

The Homosexuality Issue

Homosexuality is another extremely divisive issue within Christianity, but not the question of whether a homosexual can be a Christian. Society's more liberal attitudes toward homosexuality are reflected within Christian churches, the vast majority of which—even though they may think homosexuality wrong — say Jesus calls on his followers to minister to all people. The key question, rather, is whether an admitted, active homosexual can be a member of the clergy or serve in other leadership roles.

Only a few of the most liberal Christian churches, such as the Unitarian Universalist and the United Church of Christ, openly admit homosexual clergy. Most others specifically bar homosexuals, although there are doubtless many individual members of the clergy who are not open about their homosexuality. The issue was brought into sharp focus in 2003 when the bishops of the Episcopal Church of the United States voted to approve the ordination of an avowed homosexual, the Right Reverend Gene Robinson, as bishop of New Hampshire.

Opponents of homosexual clergy point out that ordaining homosexuals is different from ordaining women, because homosexuality is specifically banned by the Bible. For example, Jewish law, as set forth in the Old Testament book of Leviticus, condemns homosexuality, and Paul, in Romans 1:26–27, writes of "dishonorable passions" and "men committing shameless acts with men and receiving in their own persons the due penalty for their error." Thus, opponents say, homosexuals, while they may be ministered to, are not worthy to become ministers. One of the opponents' most vehement spokesmen, the Right Reverend Jack Iker, bishop of the Episcopal Diocese of Fort Worth, said,

Gene Robinson, an avowed homosexual, is pictured here at his ordination as bishop of New Hampshire, an act that threatened to split the Episcopal Church of the United States.

These decisions have divided and broken the Church we love and serve. . . . We will not accede to them. . . . We must say that they are contrary to the Holy Scriptures and to the clear moral teaching of the Church. . . . The Church cannot condone fornication or sexual relationships between members of the same sex. For this reason, it is wrong for the Church to ordain a practicing homosexual.[42]

The Liberal Argument

Those who condone the ordination of homosexual clergy argue that only Jesus was supposedly free of all sin and thus all ministers are sinners in some respect. Why, they ask, single out homosexuality? Others advocate something of a middle course.

Doug Nave, a Presbyterian Church (USA) lay leader arguing for a narrowly defeated amendment that would have allowed such ordination in 2001, said, "No home should force a choice between authenticity and inclusion; but our family home, the Presbyterian Church, does just that . . . and so people leave home. . . . This issue is not important enough to split our family. Perhaps we should say what Jesus said about homosexuality: nothing."[43] Moderates within most of the affected denominations sought to find what Reverend Susan Andrews, moderator of the Presbyterian Church (USA), called a "middle way,"[44] whereby individual churches or groups could follow their own consciences on the matter.

The controversy, however, does threaten to divide Christianity. Conservative dioceses have already threatened to split from the main body of the American Episcopal Church. Some churches within the Presbyterian Church (USA) say they

A Call for Reconciliation

In 2003 the Episcopal Church in the United States was deeply divided over the ordination as bishop of New Hampshire of an avowed homosexual, the Right Reverend Gene Robinson. Some dioceses, areas under the control of individual bishops, threatened to withdraw from the church. One bishop, Right Reverend Carolyn Tanner Irish of Utah, issued this plea for reconciliation, found at www.episcopal-ut.org:

"Our church is, and has always been, the most comprehensive of Christian families, because we have sought to embrace theological and cultural diversity of the kind that has sometimes fractured other Protestant churches. Presently the issue of homosexuality has put us on a global and very public stage, but that appears to be the really new element in our situation, not the challenge of abiding in our differences. Indeed, more than abiding.

"Reconciliation is the mission of God in this world, through his son, Jesus Christ. It is for that reconciliation which we must now pray. Opinions, after all, are not ultimate. Love is ultimate.

"As God loves Bishop Gene Robinson, God also loves the majority and the minority who voted last summer. And it is God's love, after all, that creates and sustains our communion with him and with one another."

will do the same if the denomination sanctions homosexual ordination. The United Methodist Church in 2004 faced similar issues when it challenged the ordination of an openly lesbian minister.

The Specter of Abuse

The sexual orientation of clergy is also a major issue in the Roman Catholic Church, which in the United States suffered a major scandal over the sexual abuse of children —most often boys—by priests. After months of allegations and lawsuits, a report commissioned by the church and released in February 2004 said that 4,392 Catholic priests—about 4 percent of the total in the United States—had been involved in child sexual abuse from 1950 to 2002. The scandal cost the Catholic Church millions of dollars in damage claims and led to the resignation of several high church leaders who had been accused of covering up the alleged abuses.

Some Catholics, both priests and lay persons, place part of the blame on the church's mandate that priests be celibate. Depriving priests of the normal relationships their married Protestant colleagues enjoy may, they say, cause them to turn in less accepted directions for sexual grat-

ification. One suggested answer to the child abuse problem—and the issue of the steady and dramatic decline in the number of Catholic priests—is to open the priesthood to women and to allow clergy to marry. Both options, however, have been steadfastly opposed by the current pope, John Paul II.

Christian Activism

Another set of challenges facing Christianity are those it has taken upon itself—a social and political activism not seen since the days when popes regularly intervened in the affairs of kings. The principal difference is that instead of mediating between rulers, Christian activists today are battling the status quo, taking up the causes of those they feel are poor or oppressed. Not content only to provide prayer and physical aid, they have climbed into the political arena, sometimes putting their own lives at risk.

This activism goes by the general name of "liberation theology," although that term is technically applied only to efforts in Latin America. In the wider sense, however, many Christians have marshaled their forces on behalf of the homeless, oppressed minorities, the environment, victims of disease, the unborn, and many other causes.

In so doing, modern activists face a challenge in going beyond the traditional Christian roles of charity and the alleviation of suffering. Oxford University's Basil Mitchell writes, "The underlying problems of poverty and hunger are seen ultimately to require political and economic solutions. . . . It has always been a problem for Christianity how to accommodate itself to the political order."[45]

Christians, sometimes ignoring the separation of church and state, have thus inserted themselves directly into the political process. In Latin America, Roman Catholic clergy—often against the wishes of their national leaders and the Vatican—have given direct aid to rebels in armed struggle against a central government. This aid has included everything from providing hiding places to donating funds ultimately used to buy weapons.

The Church and Solidarity

Activist Catholics in Latin America often have found themselves in the odd position of supporting Communists, who in theory oppose religion having any role in society. On the other hand, the Roman Catholic Church played a large role in the overthrow of communism in Europe. Although the Polish labor movement Solidarity may have actually begun the entire process, there was a huge undercurrent of religious fervor sparked by the visit to Poland of Pope John Paul II, a native of that country. Zbigniew Brzezinski, who was national security adviser to U.S. president Jimmy Carter, wrote, "Its Roman Catholic religion, which sets Poland apart from its immediate neighbors and traditional enemies, served to reinforce the sense of nationalism and imbue it with a doctrinal content directly at variance with communism."[46]

In the United States, conservative Protestant churches have been the most politically active. In 1979 the Reverend Jerry Falwell founded the Moral Majority, a nationwide organization of conservative Christians whose expressed purpose was to pursue a political agenda. The Moral Majority's influence is sometimes credited with the election of President Ronald Reagan in 1980 and almost certainly was a large factor in the shift from Democratic Party to Republican Party control in the southern states, where fundamentalist Christians are most numerous.

More recently, conservative political groups have had less success on national and state levels and have concentrated more on local races.

Pope John Paul II celebrates mass during a 1983 visit to his native Poland. The pope's visits helped to bolster the Polish anti-Communist labor movement.

Some have chosen to run candidates for local and state school boards in pursuit of religious goals, such as to limit the teaching of evolution in biology classes.

Social Movements

The involvement of conservative Christians in American politics cannot obscure Christians' direct in-volvement in liberal causes, how-ever. One of the best examples is the civil rights movement in the United States. Ever since the Reverend Martin Luther King Jr. founded the Southern Christian Leadership Conference in 1957, African American ministers and their Anglo counterparts have been at the fore-front of the movement. Like the more political activists, they have adopted a tactic of direct confrontation, but of a nonviolent nature. Addressing those who opposed black civil rights, King wrote:

> We will match your capacity to inflict suffering with our capacity to endure suffering. We will meet your physical force with soul force. We will not hate you, but we will not obey your evil laws. We will soon wear you down by our capacity to suffer. So in winning the victory we will not only win freedom for ourselves, but we will so appeal to your heart and conscience that you will be changed also.[47]

On the opposite end of the political spectrum, conservative Christians have adopted some of the same tactics in demonstrating their opposition to abortion. They have staged protests at state capitols, courthouses, and—most dramatically—clinics and hospitals in which abortions are performed. Like some of the civil rights marches, however, these protest have sometimes turned violent as pro-life and pro-choice forces clash.

Loss of Influence

The ability of Christianity to be effective, as either a political or moral force, is being undermined by fundamental changes in society. Once the single most potent force in the world, Christianity has seen its influence steadily decline where it has traditionally been the strongest—Europe and North America. Most European countries, including even Italy, long the center of Christianity, are officially nonsectarian. In Great Britain, one country that does have an official religion in the Church of England, that religion is largely ignored. Only one of every ten persons attends a Christian service other than a wedding or funeral.

Christianity shows signs of more vitality in the United States. Membership is increasing, and the rate of church attendance is about four times that of Europe. The principal Protestant denominations, however, have seen a membership decline of about 13 percent in the last ten years, according to the Barna Research Group. At the same time, the more fundamentalist groups, such as the Assemblies of God and Pentecostals, have increased, in some cases by more than 50 percent. Roman Catholic membership has increased as well, in some measure due to emigration from Latin America, where Catholics form a large majority.

In both Europe and the United States, however, Christians make up less of the population than before. Emigration from Asia, North Africa, and the Middle East has vastly increased the numbers of non-Christians. Thus it is that many a medium-sized city in the American Midwest now has an Islamic mosque and a Buddhist temple to go along with the Christian churches and Jewish synagogues.

Loss of Authority

Western Christianity has seen not only its numerical superiority diminish but also its control over its members lessen. Adherence to doctrine—Queen Elizabeth I's "trifles" —has given way to following one's individual conscience. Increasingly, Christians listen to what their church teaches, then decide for themselves which teachings should be followed.

This is especially true for Roman Catholics, who as recently as the 1950s were threatened with damnation if they strayed from church dogma. Today's Catholics, particularly in the United States, pick and choose, giving rise to the term "cafeteria Catholics."

As reliance on doctrine has declined, so has the distinction among Christian groups. "As modern societies came to function with diminished regard for religion," writes Oxford sociologist Bryan Wilson, "private individuals also ceased to reinforce their own identity in specifically religious terms: Baptist or Methodist, and eventually Anglican or even Roman Catholic, became labels with diminishing differentiation."[48]

It was logical and perhaps inevitable, therefore, that Christians would seek to reverse the centuries-old trend of division and try to once more become Paul's "one faith." The World Council of Churches (WCC), founded in 1948, now includes almost 350 church groups, denominations, and fellowships, including most Protestant denominations and the Orthodox churches. The WCC preaches no doctrine but instead concentrates on fostering cooperation among churches, encouraging interchurch study, and providing aid to refugees.

The WCC, however, is not inclusive of Christianity. The Roman Catholic Church is not a member, although it works with the WCC on occasional projects. In addition, many of the most conservative American denominations, including the Southern Baptists, have rejected the WCC as being too liberal.

Vatican II

The Roman Catholic Church has made major strides over the last half century in reaching out to fellow Christians. The Second Vatican Council, summoned by Pope John XXIII in 1962, relaxed the Catholic view on Protestants that had been in force since the Council of Trent in the 1500s. "After centuries of refusing to deal with the challenges of the modern world by any other means than confrontation and condemnation, it [the Catholic Church] has opened itself to a dialogue with that world," historian Justo Gonzáles writes. "As a result of that dialogue, Catholics as well as Protestants and even non-Christians have been surprised to find in the Catholic Church an energy that few suspected it had."[49]

The liberalization of the Catholic Church, however, has gone only so far. Non-Catholics were disappointed when, in September 2000, the Vatican published a document, *Dominus Iesus*, which said that all other Christian churches are in a "gravely deficient situation in comparison with those who, in the

A Call for Ecumenicalism

The Roman Catholic Church, even though it made much progress toward ecumenicalism, or unity among churches and religions, as a result of the Vatican II conference, still stands aloof from such groups as the World Council of Churches. However, in 2003, the Pax Romana, a group of European Catholic professionals and intellectuals, issued a call for greater understanding among churches. This excerpt is found at www.pax romana.org:

"Religious Europe has a great need for brotherly understanding emerging from a fundamental anthropocentric dialogue between the great religious systems. Christianity—indivisible from the European experience—must now take the step towards ecumenicalism, going beyond the human threshold of particularisms, in a common faith, a shared hope and a mutual love between the traditions that go to make it up. In the whole of Europe, we must search ceaselessly for a deep agreement between the religious and spiritual dimension of human beings on the one hand, and their social and political dimension on the other, in the conviction that it is from the standpoint of conscience that we rediscover the necessary criteria to apply to social, cultural and political values."

The Second Vatican Council, summoned by Pope John XXIII (left), relaxed many restrictions of the Roman Catholic Church.

[Catholic] Church, have the fullness of the means of salvation."[50]

Difficulties thus remain, on the part of Catholic, Protestant, and Orthodox churches, before Christianity can present a united front against today's problems. Perhaps the greatest challenge to Christianity since its very existence was threatened by Roman persecutions is to prevent further fragmentation into ever more numerous sects and denominations and to remain a relevant force in today's ever more secular world. As Father Vincent Donovan, a Roman Catholic missionary, writes:

> What we are coming to see now is that there must be many responses possible to the Christian message, which have hitherto been neither encouraged nor allowed. We have come to believe that any valid, positive response to the Christian message could and should be recognized and accepted as such. That is the church that might have been, and might yet be.[51]

Notes

Chapter 1: Jesus of Nazareth

1. Roland Herbert Bainton, *The Horizon History of Christianity*. New York: American Heritage, 1964, p. 47.
2. Gerald Hall, "How Do We Interpret the Parables and Miracles of Jesus," www.dilibrary.ecu.edu.au.
3. John Dominic Crosson, *The Historical Jesus: The Life of a Mediterranean Jewish Peasant*. San Francisco: HarperSanFrancisco, 1992, p. 287.
4. Hall, "How Do We Interpret the Parables."
5. Bruce L. Shelly, *Church History in Plain Language*. Nashville, TN: Thomas Nelson, 1982, p. 7.
6. Alan Scholes, "Why Did Jesus Die?" www.leaderu.com.

Chapter 3: Persecution to Prominence

7. Quoted in Justo L. González, *The Story of Christianity, vol. 1, The Early Church to the Dawn of the Reformation*. San Francisco: HarperSanFrancisco, 1984, p. 75.
8. Quoted in Bainton, *The Horizon History of Christianity*, p. 70.
9. Quoted in González, *The Story of Christianity*, vol. 1, p. 35.
10. Quoted in Philip Schaff, *History of the Christian Church*, www.ccel.org.
11. Quoted in James Lees-Milne, *St. Peter's*. Boston: Little, Brown, 1966, p. 44.
12. Quoted in Brian Moynahan, *The Faith: A History of Christianity*. New York: Doubleday, 2002, p. 96.
13. González, *The Story of Christianity*, vol. 1, p. 122.
14. Quoted in Philip Schaff, *Eusebius Pamphilius: Church History, Life of Constantine, Oration in Praise of Constantine*, www.ccel.org.

Chapter 4: Heresy and Schism

15. Quoted in González, *The Story of Christianity*, vol. 1, p. 161.
16. Quoted in Moynahan, *The Faith*, p. 123.
17. Quoted in Bainton, *The Horizon History of Christianity*, p. 101.
18. Quoted in Moynahan, *The Faith*, p. 121.
19. Quoted in Moynahan, *The Faith*, p. 123.
20. Moynahan, *The Faith*, p. 213.

Chapter 5: Power and Perversion

21. Quoted in Moynahan, *The Faith*, p. 195.
22. Quoted in González, *The Story of Christianity*, vol. 1, p. 311.

Chapter 6: Reformation and Counter-Reformation

23. Quoted in Justo L. González, *The Story of Christianity*, vol. 2, *The Reformation to the Present Day*, p. 19.
24. Quoted in Patrick Colinson, "The Late Medieval Church and Its

Reformation," in John McManners,
ed., *The Oxford History of Christianity*.
Oxford: Oxford University Press,
1990, p. 260.
25. Quoted in González, *The Story of
Christianity*, vol. 2, p. 28.
26. Quoted in "John Calvin: Theologian
and Ecclesiastical Statesman,"
www.hfac.uh.edu.
27. Quoted in McManners, "Enlightenment: Secular and Christian," in *The
Oxford History of Christianity*, p. 260.
28. Quoted in McManners, "Enlightenment: Secular and Christian," p. 285.

Chapter 7: Expansion and Enlightenment
29. Quoted in Moynahan, *The Faith*,
p. 506.
30. Quoted in Moynahan, *The Faith*,
p. 511.
31. Quoted in Arthur Helps, *The Spanish
Conquest in America and Its Relation to
the History of Slavery and to the Government of Colonies*, www.albion.edu.
32. Quoted in Moynahan, *The Faith*,
p. 507.
33. "About Unitarian Universalism," www.
uua.org.
34. Quoted in Moynahan, *The Faith*,
p. 587.

Chapter 8: Beliefs and Worship
35. "Elizabeth I—Quotes," www.eliza
bethi.org.
36. Episcopal Church of the United
States, *Book of Common Prayer*, 1982.
www.stpeters.org.

37. Maurice Wiles, "What Christians
Believe," in *The Oxford History of
Christianity*, p. 575.
38. Quoted in Bainton, *The Horizon
History of Christianity*, p. 362.
39. Episcopal Church of the United
States, *Book of Common Prayer*.

Chapter 9: Christianity in the New Millennium
40. Ruth Brandon Minter, "Hidden
Dynamics Block Women's Access to
Pulpits," *Christian Century*, August
29–September 5, 1984. www.religion
online.org.
41. Patricia David, "The Role of
Women in the Church." www.zhills
wesley.org.
42. Jack Iker, "Bishop Iker's Address to
Delegates of the Special Convention
of the Diocese of Fort Worth,"
September 30, 2003. www.american
anglican.org.
43. Doug Nave, "The Presbyterian
Church (USA) and Gay/Lesbian
Ordination: Year 2001 and 2002
Events." www.religioustolerance.org.
44. Susan Andrews, "The Presbyterian
Church (USA) and Gay-Lesbian
Ordination." on www.religioustoler
ance.org.
45. Basil Mitchell, "The Christian
Conscience," in *The Oxford History
of Christianity*, p. 633.
46. Zbigniew Brzezinski, "How Solidarity
Arose," *Hoover Digest*, no. 1, 2000.
www.hooverdigest.org/001/brzez
inski.html.

47. Martin Luther King Jr., "To Chester Bowles: 28 October 1957," *The Papers of Martin Luther King, Jr.*, www.stanford.edu.

48. Bryan Wilson, "New Images of Christian Community," in *The Oxford History of Christianity*, p. 599.

49. González, *The Story of Christianity*, vol. 2, p. 359.

50. Congregation for the Doctrine of the Faith, *Dominus Iesus*, August 6, 2000. www.vatican.va.

51. Quoted in John Taylor, "The Future of Christianity," in *The Oxford History of Christianity*, p. 682.

For Further Reading

Books

Richard P. Heitzenrater, *Wesley and the People Called Methodists*. Nashville, TN: Abingdon, 1995. Well-written and easily understandable work dealing not only with John Wesley's life but with his philosophy that shaped the modern Methodist Church and much of Protestant Christianity.

James Janda, *Inigo: The Life of St. Ignatius Loyola for Young Readers*. Mahwah, NJ: Paulist, 1995. Highly readable biography of the founder of the Society of Jesus written from a Roman Catholic point of view.

Frederick Nohl, *Luther: Biography of a Reformer*. St. Louis, MO: Concordia, 2003. Originally published in 1962, this entertaining biography was rereleased in conjunction with the motion picture *Luther* and includes photographs from the film.

Mark A. Noll. *Protestants in America*. Oxford: Oxford University Press Children's, 2000. Part of the Religion in America series, this book does a good job of covering a vast amount of data—from the Puritans to the Moral Majority—in a concise space.

Web Sites

Christian History and Biography (www.christianitytoday.com). Packed not only with articles on church history, but also with news stories on contemporary topics in Christianity.

Religion Online (www.religion-online.org). Wonderful source of Internet links to individual denominational sites, articles on a wide range of subjects, and full-text works on Christianity—all from a nonsectarian point of view.

Works Consulted

Books

Roland Herbert Bainton, *The Horizon History of Christianity*. New York: American Heritage, 1964. Beautifully illustrated and yet highly informative account of Christianity from the ministry of Jesus to the present day.

David W. Bercot, ed., *The Dictionary of Early Church Beliefs*. Peabody, MA: Hendrickson, 1998. Nicely arranged guide to all the philosophies, heresies, and theologies of the early centuries of Christianity.

John Dominic Crossan, *The Historical Jesus: The Life of a Mediterranean Jewish Peasant*. San Francisco, CA: HarperSanFrancisco, 1992. The author examines the life and works of Jesus from several standpoints—revolutionary, magician, messiah, healer, teacher—against the historical background of the time.

Richard Fletcher, *The Cross and the Crescent*. New York: Viking, 2003. History of the interaction between Christianity and Islam from the rise of Muhammad to the Protestant Reformation.

Justo L. González, *The Story of Christianity*. 2 vols. San Francisco: HarperSanFrancisco, 1984. Massive (more than 800 pages) history of Christianity in two volumes—*The Early Church to the Dawn of the Reformation* and *The Reformation to the Present Day*—in which the author does a nice job of explaining abstract theology in an understandable manner.

Roy Hattersley, *The Life of John Wesley*. New York: Doubleday, 2003. This biography of the founder of Methodism portrays Wesley in a somewhat unfavorable light as a rigid conservative.

Paul Johnson, *A History of Christianity*. New York: Touchstone, 1995. Very comprehensive history, but readability is hindered by page after page of text unrelieved by pictures or illustrations.

James Lees-Milne, *St. Peter's*. Boston: Little, Brown, 1966. Written by a well-known English architectural historian, this is one of the most comprehensive and readable accounts available of the development of Saint Peter's basilica.

Alister E. McGrath, ed., *The Church Theology Reader*. Malden, MA: Blackwell, 2001. Writings through the ages on Christianity arranged under major headings such as "Doctrine of God," "Person of Christ," "Human Nature," and "The Sacraments."

John McManners, ed., *The Oxford History of Christianity*. Oxford: Oxford University Press, 1990. Collection of nineteen essays by scholars from around the world on various aspects of Christianity throughout its history.

Brian Moynahan, *The Faith: A History of Christianity*. New York: Doubleday, 2002. Comprehensive and highly readable account of Christianity enlivened with liberal use of quotations of major figures in church history.

Bruce L. Shelly, *Church History in Plain Language*. Nashville, TN: Thomas Nelson, 1982. Arranged under eight major headings, this history does a good job of explaining extremely involved theological issues.

Internet Sources

Susan Andrews, "The Presbyterian Church (USA) and Gay-Lesbian Ordination," www.religioustolerance.org.

Anonymous, "The Apostles' Creed," www.creeds.net.

Augustine of Hippo, *The City of God,* http://ccat.sas.upenn.edu.

Baptist Faith and Steering Committee, *Baptist Faith and Message*. Nashville, TN: 2000, www.sbc.net.

St. Benedict, *The Rule of St. Benedict,* www.osb.org.

Pope Boniface VIII, "Unam Sanctam," 1302. www.fordham.edu.

William J. Bouwsma, "John Calvin: Theologian and Ecclesiastical Statesman," www.hfac.uh.edu.

"British Clergy Have Doubts About Virgin Birth," *Sydney Morning Herald*, December 23, 2000. www.wmh.com.

Zbigniew Brzezinski, "How Solidarity Arose," *Hoover Digest*, no. 1, 2000. www.hooverdigest.org/001/brzezinski.html.

Celsus, *True Word*, www.emporia.edu.

Congregation for the Doctrine of the Faith, *Dominus Iesus*, August 6, 2000. www.vatican.va.

Council of Trent, "Canons on Justification," http://ic.net.

John Cummings, *The Voyage of Christopher Columbus: Columbus' Own Journal of Discovery Newly Restored and Translated*, www.princeton.edu.

Patricia David, "The Role of Women in the Church," www.zhillswesley.org.

Jonathan Edwards, "Sinners in the Hands of an Angry God," www.jonathanedwards.com.

"Elizabeth I—Quotes," www.elizabethi.org.

Episcopal Church of the United States, *Book of Common Prayer*, 1982. www.stpeters.org.

Gerald Hall, "How Do We Interpret the Parables and Miracles of Jesus," www.dllibrary.ccu.edu.au.

Paul Halsall, ed., *Internet Medieval Sourcebook*. New York: Fordham University, 1996. www.fordham.edu/halsall/sbook.html.

Arthur Helps, *The Spanish Conquest in America and Its Relation to the History of Slavery and to the Government of Colonies*, www.albion.edu.

History of the Christian Church, www.ccel.org.

William E. Hull, "Women and the Southern Baptist Convention," June 18, 2000. www.christianethicstoday.com.

Jack Iker, "Bishop Iker's Address to Delegates of the Special Convention of the Diocese of Fort Worth," September 30, 2003. www.americananglican.org.

Carolyn Tanner Irish, "Statement of the Right Rev. Carolyn Tanner Irish, Bishop of Utah, on the Consecration of the Right Rev. Gene Robinson, Bishop Coadjutor-elect, Episcopal Diocese of New Hampshire," www.episcopal-ut.org.

"John Calvin: Theologian and Ecclesiastical Statesman," www.hfac.uh.edu.

Colette Joyce, "Why I'm Writing," December 1999. www.womenpriests.org.

Martin Luther King Jr., "To Chester Bowles: 28 October 1957," *The Papers of Martin Luther King, Jr.*, www.stanford.edu.

Bartolome de Las Casas, "A Brief Account of the Destruction of the Indies," www.americanjourney.psmedia.com.

St. Ignatius Loyola, "The Society's Duty to Oppose Heresy," www.georgetown.edu.

Martin Luther, "Introduction to St. Paul's Letter to the Romans," www.icl.net.org.

Mathetes, "The Epistle of Mathetes to Diognetus," www.earlychristianwriting.com.

Ruth Brandon Minter, "Hidden Dynamics Block Women's Access to Pulpits," *Christian Century*, August 29–September 5, 1984. www.religion-online.org.

Doug Nave, "The Presbyterian Church (USA) and Gay/Lesbian Ordination: Year 2001 and 2002 Events." www.religioustolerance.org.

Pax Romana International Catholic Movement for Intellectual and Cultural Affairs, "Luxembourg European Declaration," www.paxromana.org.

William Hickling Prescott, *The History of the Conquest of Mexico*, www.xroads.virginia.edu.

Bruce A. Robinson, "Female Clergy in Eastern Orthodox Churches, Protestant Denominations, and Other Religions." Kingston: Ontario Consultants on Religious Tolerance, 1998.

Philip Schaff, *Eusebius Pamphilius: Church History, Life of Constantine, Oration in Praise of Constantine*, www.ccel.org.

———, *History of the Christian Church*, www.ccel.org.

Alan Scholes, "Why Did Jesus Die?" www.leaderu.com.

James M. Stalker, *The Life of St. Paul*, www.tks.org.

St. Symeon, "On God as a Mystery," www.ocl.org.

Tacitus, "Nero's Persecution of the Christians," www.wsu.edu.

Thomas Aquinas, *Summa Contra Gentiles*, www.nd.edu.

Unitarian Universalist Association, "About Unitarian Universalism," www.uua.org.

John Wesley, "By Grace Are Ye Saved Through Faith," June 18, 1738. www.godrules.net.

George Whitefield, "The Good Shepherd," August 30, 1769. www.oakharbor.net.

Roger Williams, *The Bloudy Tenet of Persecution, for the Cause of Conscience. Discussed in a Conference Between Truth and Peace*, 1644. www.worldpolicy.org.

Index

abortion, 113
Abraham, 6
activism, Christian, 110–13
Africa, Christianity in, 80–81
Alexander (bishop), 46
Alexander the Great, 9
Alexander VI (pope), 81, 82
almah (young woman), 11
Ananias, 27
Andrew, Saint, 17
Andrews, Susan, 109
Anglican church. *See* Church of
    England
Apollo (Greek god), 38
apostles, the, 16–18, 21, 22–24
Apostles' Creed, 44–45, 93–98
Arianism, 46–49
Aristotle, 62, 87
Arius (priest), 46
Asia, Christianity in, 81–82
Assemblies of God, 113
Assyrian Empire, 7
Attila the Hun, 50
Augustine, Saint, 56, 57, 58, 60
Augustinian order, 71
Avignon, popes in, 66

Babylonian Captivity, 66
Babylonian Empire, 7–8
Bainton, Roland Herbert, 12, 52
Baltimore, Lord, 87
baptism, 12, 24, 98, 99, 100
Baptists, 74, 86
    see also Southern Baptist
        Convention
barbarian invasions, 50, 57, 59
Barnabas, Saint, 27
Barna Reseach Group, 113
Bartholomew, Saint, 17
Basil, Saint, 41, 49
Benedict of Nursia, Saint, 41, 42
Benedict XII (pope), 66
betulah (virgin), 11
Bible, the, 15, 34, 69
bishops, 34, 64, 75
Bloudy Tenet, The (Williams), 86
body, resurrection of, 95–96, 98
Boniface VII (pope), 65, 66
Brazil, 81

Brown, Antoinette, 104
Brzezinski, Zbigniew, 111
Byzantine Empire, 55

cafeteria Catholics, 114
Caiaphas, 19
Calvin, John, 72, 73, 74, 75
Calvinism, 72–74
Catholic Church. *See* Roman
    Catholic Church
celibacy, 61, 110
Chalcedon, Council of, 49
chapels, 39
Charlemagne (Holy Roman
    emperor), 60–61
Charles I (king of England), 78,
    87
Charles V (Holy Roman emper-
    or), 71
Charles IX (king of France), 77
Charles Martel, 53
Christ, the, 29
    see also Jesus of Nazareth
Christians, declining numbers of,
    113–14
church, Christian
    denominations of, 103, 114,
        116
    founding of, 23–24
    growth of, 34–35, 80, 87
    influence of, 114
    Judaism and, 24–25, 30
    organization, 34, 40
    Paul of Tarsus and, 27–28
church and state, 52, 57, 59–60,
    68, 78, 79
churches, building of, 37, 39–40
Church of England
    American colonies and, 85, 86
    British Empire and, 82
    Eucharist and, 102
    founding of, 74
    Methodism and, 90
    sacraments of, 99
    virgin birth and, 11
    see also Episcopal Church
Church of St. Thomas (India), 80
Church Theology Reader, The
    (McGrath), 14

Cistercian order, 61
City of God, The (Augustine), 57,
    58
Clement V (pope), 66
clergy
    celibacy and, 61, 110
    homosexuality and, 107–10
    married, 54
    ranks of, 34, 40
    women, 104–107
Clovis (Frankish king), 57
Cluniacs, 61
collection plates, 101
Columbus, Christopher, 82
commandments, 15
Communion. *See* Eucharist, the
communism, 111
confession. *See* penance
confirmation, 98
Congo, the, 81
Congregational Church, 74, 104
conscience, individual, 114
Constantine (Roman emperor),
    35–36, 37–38, 44, 46, 47
Constantinople, 37, 55
Constantinople, Council of, 51
consubstantiation, 72, 102
conversion. *See* missionaries
Coptic Church, 80
corruption, 61, 66
Counter-Reformation, 74–76
Crosson, John, 14
crucifixion, the, 20–21

David (king of Israel), 6
David, Patricia, 107
deacons, 24, 34
Decius (Roman emperor), 31
deism, 87–88
Descartes, René, 62, 87
Diocletian (Roman emperor), 31
disciples, the. *See* apostles, the
Dominic, Saint, 62
Dominican order, 62
Dominus Iesus (papal publication),
    115–16
Domitian (Roman emperor), 31
Donovan, Vincent, 116
dyophysites, 49, 50

Eastern Church. *See* Orthodox Church

"Ecclesiastical Ordinances" (Calvin), 73

ecumenicalism, 114, 115

Edict of Milan, 36–37

education, 43, 62, 74–75, 112

elect, the. *See* predestination

Elizabeth I (queen of England), 93, 114

encomienda (assignment), 82

Episcopal Church, 74, 100–102, 103, 107, 109

epistles, 28

Eucharist, the
Jesus' presence in, 72
liturgy of, 101–102
origin of, 19, 30
Photian Schism and, 54
as sacrament, 98, 99

Europe, modern, 113–14

Eusebius of Caesarea, 35, 36, 38–39, 47

Eutyches, 49

Evangelical Movement, 91–92, 101

excommunication, 64

extreme unction, 98

faith, 28, 62, 63, 68, 69

Falwell, Jerry, 111

Fox, George, 89

France, 66, 77, 84–85

Franciscan order, 62

Francis of Assisi, Saint, 62

Frederick the Wise, 71

freedom, religious. *See* toleration, religious

Galileo, 74

Genesis, book of, 6

Geneva (Switzerland), 73–74

Geneva Confession, 75

Gentiles, Christianity and, 24

"Gloria Patri," 100

Gnosticism, 44, 48

God, nature of, 28, 45–46, 48–49, 93–95

God's love, 15–16

González, Justo L., 47, 115

"Good Shepherd, The" (Whitefield), 91

gospels, 10, 11, 19, 34

Great Awakening, 91–92, 101

Great Britain, 85, 113

Great Western Schism, 66

Gregory I (pope), 59–60

Gregory VII (pope), 64, 65

Gregory XI (pope), 66

Hall, Gerald, 12–13, 16

Halsall, Paul, 50

Hapsburg, house of, 78

healing, 18–19

heaven, 96

Hebrew people, 6

hell, 96–97

Henry III (Holy Roman emperor), 62

Henry IV (Holy Roman emperor), 64–65

Henry V (Holy Roman emperor), 65

Henry VIII (king of England), 74

heresy and schism
Arianism, 46–49
Dominican order and, 62
Gnosticism, 44
Great Western Schism, 66
Inquisition and, 74
Photian Schism, 54–55

Holy Roman Empire, 60–61, 62, 64–66, 78

Holy Spirit, 10, 95

Holy Trinity. *See* Trinity, the

homilies, 101

homosexuality, 107–10

Horizon History of Christianity, The (Bainton), 52

Hosius (bishop), 46

Humbert (cardinal), 54–55

Hume, David, 62

Ignatius of Loyola, Saint, 75

Ignatius (patriarch), 54

Iker, Jack, 107–108

Indians, conversion of, 82–85

indulgences, 67, 70, 75

Industrial Revolution, 90

inner light, 89

Innocent III (pope), 65–66

Inquisition, the, 74

Internet Medieval Sourcebook, 50

"Introduction to St. Paul's Letter to the Romans" (Luther), 69

Ireland, monks in, 42, 43

Irish, Carolyn Tanner, 109

Isaiah (prophet), 8–9, 11, 12, 21

Islam, 53, 55

Israel, kingdom of, 7

Israelites, 6–7

Italy, 113

Jacob, 6

James the Greater, Saint, 17, 30

James the Lesser, Saint, 17

Jesuits, 74–75, 81–82

Jesus of Nazareth
apostles of, 16–18, 22–24
baptism of, 12
birth of, 10, 11, 12
death of, 19–21
historical evidence for, 14
ministry of, 12–13, 16
miracles of, 18–19
nature of, 45–46, 48–49, 94–95
rationalism and, 88–89

John, book of, 96

John, Saint (apostle), 10, 17

John Paul II (pope), 110, 111

John the Baptist, 12

John XII (pope), 61

John XXIII (pope), 115

Joyce, Colette, 106

Judah, kingdom of, 7

Judaism
early Christianity and, 24
Jesus of Nazareth and, 16–17
law and, 14–15
liturgy and, 99, 100
origin of, 7
Zealots and, 20

Judas Iscariot, 17, 20

Jude, Saint, 17

Judea, kingdom of, 9

judgment, final, 97–98

Julius II (pope), 67

Justinian (Roman emperor), 50–52

Justin Martyr, Saint, 32, 99

Kant, Immanuel, 62

King, Martin Luther, Jr., 112, 113

Kingdom of God, 13–15, 23

knowledge, preservation of, 42, 43

Knox, John, 74
Kyrie Eleison, 100–101

Lactantius (writer), 35
Las Casas, Bartolomé de, 84
last rites, 98
Last Supper, the, 19, 30
  see also Eucharist, the
Lateran Synod, 52
Latin America, Christianity in, 82–84
law, Jewish, 8, 14–15, 28
Lazarus, 19
Leo I (pope), 49, 50
Leo III (pope), 60
Leo IX (pope), 54
liberation theology, 110, 111
Licinius, 36, 37
Life of Constantine (Eusebius), 47
Life of St. Paul, The (Stalker), 29
liturgy. See worship, forms of
Liturgy of the Eucharist, 101–102
Liturgy of the Word, 100
Locke, John, 87
Lombards, 59
Luke, Saint, 10, 11
Luther, Martin, 67, 68–70
Lutheran Church, 102

Marcus Aurelius (Roman emperor), 31
Mark, Saint, 10
marriage, 54, 98
Martin of Tours, Saint, 39
martyrdom. See persecution, religious
Mary (convent founder), 40
Mary, the Virgin, 10, 11, 94
Maryland, 87
Mary Magdalene, 21
Mason, James, 35
Massachusetts, 85–86
Mathetes (writer), 33
Matthew, gospel of, 45–46, 97
Matthew, Saint (apostle), 10, 11, 17
Maximinus, 37
McGrath, Alister, 14
Mecca, 53
messiah, the, 8, 12, 20, 29
Methodism, 90

see also United Methodist Church
Michael Cerularius, 52, 54–55
Milvan Bridge, battle of, 35
Minter, Ruth Brandon, 107
miracles, 18–19
missionaries, 80–82, 84–85
monasticism, 40–42, 61–62
monophysites, 49, 50, 51–52, 57
Moral Majority, 111
Moynahan, Brian, 55
Muhammad, Prophet, 53
mysticism, 49

Nave, Doug, 109
Nero (Roman emperor), 25, 30, 31
New Being, the, 14
New Testament. See Bible, the
Nicea, Council of, 46–48
Nicene Creed, 48, 54, 95, 101
Nicholas I (pope), 54
"Ninety-five Theses" (Luther), 70–71
nonviolent protest, 113
North America, Christianity in, 79, 84–87

Old Testament. See Bible, the
ordination, 98
original sin, 56
Orthodox Church, 49–50, 53–55, 105
orthodoxy, 44
Ortiz, Tomás, 82–84

Pachomius (monk), 40–41
pagan religions, 34, 37
pageantry, 40
papacy, the
  conversion of Indians and, 82, 83
  decline of, 61, 66–67
  divisions within, 62, 64
  Gregory I (pope) and, 59–60
  Holy Roman Empire and, 62, 64–66
  during Middle Ages, 60, 61
  power of, 49
parables, 16
Passover, 19
Paul of Tarsus

conversion of, 26–27
death of, 30
epistles of, 28
Eucharist and, 102
influence of, 28–29
orthodoxy and, 44
travels of, 27–28
women and, 106
Pax Romana, 115
peace, kiss of, 101
Peace of Nuremberg, 71
Peace of Westphalia, 78
Pelagius II (pope), 59
penance, 60, 98, 99
Penn, William, 86
Pennsylvania, Commonwealth of, 79, 86
Pentecost, 23–24
Pentecostalism, 92, 103, 113
persecution, religious, 25, 31–32, 85–86
Persecutions of Diocletian, The (Mason), 35
Peter, Saint, 17, 24, 49, 82
Pharisees, 17, 19
Philip, Saint, 17
Philip IV (king of France), 66
philosophy, 62
Photian Schism, 54–55
Photius (patriarch), 54
Pietism, 89
Pilate, Pontius, 20–21
pluralism, 66–67, 75
politics, 65–66, 104, 110–12
Pompey (Roman general), 9
popes, 34
Portugal, 80–82
predestination, 28–29, 72, 92
Presbyterian Church, 109–10
Presbyterianism, 74
priests. See clergy
printing press, 71
prophecy, Old Testament, 8–9, 12
Protestantism, branches of, 71–72, 74
Protestant Reformation, 67, 70–71, 87
purgatory, 60, 97, 98
Puritanism, 74, 85–86

Quakerism, 86, 90, 102–103

rationalism, 87–89

Reagan, Ronald, 111
reason, 62, 63
  see also rationalism
Recared (Visigoth king), 57
Reformation. *See* Protestant
  Reformation
Requerimiento (Requirement), 82
resurrection
  of Jesus, 21, 95, 97
  of the dead, 95–97
Revelations, book of, 34, 96–97
Rhode Island, 86
Robinson, Gene, 107, 109
Roman Catholic Church
  authority of, 56, 60, 62, 64,
    65–66, 114
  corruption in, 61, 66
  Counter-Reformation and,
    74–76
  final judgment and, 97–98
  in Latin America, 84, 110,
    111
  liturgy, 100, 101
  in North America, 85, 87, 113
  Photian Schism and, 54–55
  sacraments of, 98–99
  sexual abuse and, 110
  Vatican II and, 114–16
  women clergy and, 105
  World Council of Churches
    (WCC) and, 114
  see also papacy, the
Roman Empire
  division of, 50–52
  Jesus of Nazareth and, 17,
    20–21
  official religion of, 49
  in Palestine, 9
  religious persecution, 25,
    31–33
  see also Constantine
Rome, sack of, 57, 59
Rule of St. Benedict, The, 42
rulers, secular, 58, 59
Russian Orthodox Church, 53

sabbath, 30, 99
sacraments, 70, 98–99
sacrifice, 19
Sadducees, 17
salvation, 28, 89
Sanhedrin, the, 17, 20, 24, 81

São Salvador (Congo), 81
Saul of Tarsus. *See* Paul of Tarsus
schism. *See* heresy and schism
scholastics, 62
schools, monastic, 43
Search for the Historical Jesus, The
  (Tillich), 14
Second Coming, 98
secularism, 104
sermons, 101
sexual abuse, 110
sexual revolution, 104
Shelly, Bruce, 18
Simon, Saint, 17
simony, 62, 64, 66
sin, 72
Smith, William, 92
social activism, 112–13
social order, Jesus of Nazareth
  and, 13–14, 17
Society of Friends. *See*
  Quakerism
Solidarity movement, 111
Solomon (king of Israel), 6
souls, eternal, 98
Southern Baptist Convention,
  105, 114
Southern Christian Leadership
  Conference, 112
Spanish conquest, 81, 82–84
Spiritualism, 89–90
Stalker, James M., 29
St. Bartholomew's Day Massacre,
  77
Stephen (martyr), 24–25
Stephen VI (pope), 61
Story of Christianity, The
  (González), 47
St. Peter's Basilica, 37, 67
Summa Contra Gentiles (Thomas
  Aquinas), 63
Summa Theologica (Thomas
  Aquinas), 62

Tacitus, 25, 33
Tertullian (theologian), 32, 46
Theodora (Roman empress), 51
Theodosius, 49
theology, 46, 62, 69
third race, the, 32–33
Thirty Years' War, 78
Thomas, Saint, 17

Thomas Aquinas, Saint, 62, 63,
  87
Tillich, Paul, 14
Timothy, book of, 106
Titus (emperor), 30
toleration, religious, 78–79,
  86–87
tongues, speaking in, 24, 103
transubstantiation, 72, 102
Trent, Council of, 75–76, 77, 115
Trinity, the, 45–46, 94–95

Unam Sanctam (papal bull), 65
Unitarian Universalist Church,
  74, 88, 105, 107
United Church of Christ. *See*
  Congregational Church
United Methodist Church, 110
United States, 103, 113

Valerian (Roman emperor), 31
Vandals, 57
Vatican II, 114–16
Vigilius (pope), 51, 52
virgin birth, 11, 94
virtues, 16–17
Visigoths, 57

war
  just, 57, 60
  religious, 76–78, 87, 93
wealth, 18
Wesley, Charles, 90
Wesley, John, 89–90, 92
Western Church. *See* Roman
  Catholic Church
Whitefield, George, 89, 91, 92,
  101
Wiles, Maurice, 94, 103
Williams, Roger, 85–86
Wilson, Bryan, 114
witchcraft, 18
women, 12, 104–107
Word of God. *See* Bible, the
World Council of Churches
  (WCC), 114, 115
worship, forms of, 39–40,
  99–103

Zealots, 20
Zoroastrianism, 49
Zwingli, Ulrich, 71–72

Picture Credits

About the Author

William W. Lace is a native of Fort Worth, Texas, where he is executive assistant to the chancellor at Tarrant County College. He holds a bachelor's degree from Texas Christian University, a master's degree from East Texas State, and a doctorate from the University of North Texas. Prior to joining Tarrant County College, he was director of the News Service at the University of Texas at Arlington and a writer and columnist for the *Fort Worth Star-Telegram*. He has written more than twenty-five books for Lucent, one of which—*The Death Camps*—was selected by the New York Public Library for its 1999 Recommended Teenage Reading List. He and his wife, Laura, a retired school librarian, live in Arlington, Texas, and have two children and three grandchildren.